MW00905689

TO: Mug of Woe:
Wreck the Halls

FROM: Tales that will get you
on the naughty list

EDITORS: KYLE THERESE CRANSTON JENN DLUGOS

Thanks to all of our fans of the Woe books, the writers who made this book possible, and Vikki Rush, who designed our woefully awesome cover.

Foreword

Holidays are times of joy. You play board games, chill with loved ones, and scarf down tasty treats, promising to be "good" the next day. These special days allow us to take a few precious moments and curl up by the fire with our closest brethren to wish peace on Earth and good will to men. Some people make this holiday magic effortlessly. None of those people are in this book.

At *Mug of Woe,* we are in the business of bringing you true stories of misfortune by writers and comedians from all over the world. *Wreck the Halls* is our fourth book, and we are stoked to share with you these tales of the holidays gone wrong.

It's the Most Woeful Time of the Year features tales of holiday misery and will teach you why it's a bad idea to take a bunch of 6th graders to see *The Nutcracker*.

If you've ever had a holiday party go up in flames, **Derailing the Party Bus** will boost your spirits and remind you to pack a bottle opener the next time you're tailgating.

Woe the Halls is full of not-so-fun encounters with holiday decorations, shopping, gifts, and a group of pissed-off leprechauns.

If you wish for love during the holidays, **Cupid Missed** will make you glad you're without a plus one…at least for this year.

My Special Day of Woe features birthday stories full of "woe is me" moments, including why it really sucks to be born on April Fools' Day.

Home for the Woe-i-days explains why ditching your family during the holidays is probably your best course of action, even if they offer to "host" the family dinner.

So ignore your shopping list, pour a glass of egg nog, and enjoy these woeful tales that got us on the naughty list.

Table of Contents

It's the Most Woeful Time of the Year

Derailing the Party Bus

Woe the Halls

Cupid Missed

My Special Day of Woe

Home for the Woe-i-days

SECTION ONE

It's the Most Woeful Time of the Year

Fresh Apple Pie, Sir

Maria Ciampa

The Christmas I was ten, Mom forgot to stop pouring the rum in the rum cake.

"You know how it is!" she cried, buzzing with holiday spirit and whiskey, "You start pouring the rum, and before you know it, one of the kids asks you where the batteries for the new Nintendo are, and BOOM, you empty the bottle in the cake!"

After our traditional "putting up the tree" fight, an annual event marked by yelling, tree-trunk sawing, and tinsel thrown angrily and ineffectively at one another, the alcoholic cake helped put us back in a lighter mood. Tree up and rum cake enjoyed, my sisters and I decided to make a music video to Bob Marley's "Buffalo Soldier." We set the huge camera on its tripod facing the tree, and let our choreography speak for itself. A seven-year-old Sarah did the worm on the floor, I was proud to "walk like an Egyptian," and eight-year old Chrissie showed off her signature simultaneous belly-dancing and tongue rolling, making hers the most disturbing dance of all. Mom clapped and cheered and Papa wrinkled his brow, confused at the entertainment. That Christmas we were all merrier than any other, and since then we've all held on to a touch (or more) of seasonal alcoholism.

There were holidays when siblings were splintered with restraining orders against each other. You called me a fat pig? Restraining order! You slept with my boyfriend? Restraining order! You threatened to kill me in my sleep? Restraining order! In the Ciampa family, restraining orders are a mode of communication. When you look beyond the obvious message of "stay away from me," my siblings used them to say: "Look at the drama I've created in your honor!" I came to eventually understand restraining orders for what they really are: gestures of familial love.

The phone-throwing incident happened one New Year's Eve. When attending college and graduate school in Boston, Tina, Eve, and Tony all lived together violently in my late grandmother's house, which was left to my mother. It was in the quiet suburbs of Boston, a neighborhood where people had kids and worked for the city…or for Wal-Mart. Tina got a restraining order against Tony, who reportedly threw the phone at her, shattering any sense of security she felt in his presence. In retaliation, Tony got a restraining order against Tina, calling her a "crazy bitch" who was "hell-bent on ruining his life." I was fascinated—if two people both have a restraining order against each other, do they cancel each other out? Their cohabitation made obeying that restraining order that much harder. In effect, they were both breaking the law all the time, just by being home.

There were countless Christmases when boyfriends were invited over and harassed by me and my younger sisters, a responsibility we took seriously.

"Hey Scott, did you guys French yet? Ella, did he get his spit on your face? Did he? Did you, Scotty? Wait, did you guys DO IT? Did you? Hey Scotty boy, do you have any gum? I want gum. Ooh, the insides of your pockets are warm." Before we knew it, Scott was out of the picture.

When I was 17 and Papa had been elderly as long

as I could remember, I decided it was important for us to spend time with the old man. That Thanksgiving, I rounded up Chrissie, Sarah, and Mimi, our tiny dog, to accompany Papa on what he called an "apple picking" trip. We all piled into Papa's car, which by then had been in a few accidents, including a 20-car pileup. Insurance had declared it a total loss and paid for the value of the car. Papa duct taped it, poured motor oil under the hood, and used the insurance money to proudly buy old produce labeled "Not the best, but still a good buy!"

We drove down Route 128 in Papa's jalopy, with its doors falling off and its broken spidery windshield. Over the loud roar of the engine and Mimi's incessant high-pitched barking, the AM radio blasted at a level almost audible to a deaf elderly man. Papa enjoyed the radio at this deafening volume even when the signal was lost, and we all listened to loud fizz for minutes at a time.

"Don't worry, the radio signal will return when we get out of this tunnel!" He yelled over the engine, and the barking, and the fizz, "That Click and Clack really know their stuff!"

Papa suddenly pulled over to the side of the highway and got out in the pouring rain, announcing, "Here we are!"

"I don't see any apple trees," I said.

"Of course you don't see any apple trees from here, you Banana-brain!" Papa yelled through the pouring rain. "You think the trees would just be planted by the side of the highway? Then everyone would be here!"

"Of course," I agreed, "The place would be mobbed."

Papa grabbed one of the machetes from the back of the car. Sarah held onto Mimi, both of them shivering in the cold. Chrissie stood on the rumble strip waving happily to the cars speeding by on the highway. I watched Papa get to work with his machete, cutting through the brush like he was in the jungles of South America.

Chrissie and I picked up a few machetes and went for it. Why not? We all had the same genes. We might as well enjoy them by tearing through highway side jungles north of Boston in search of free apples. When we thrashed through enough of the brush to find the apple trees, Papa acted as if he had found pirate's treasure.

"See that? All ours! Our apples!" We broke out the plastic bags and started to fill them with apples.

Then we heard Sarah, who was further in toward the highway.

"5-0! 5-0!"

Chrissie echoed, "Po-po! Po-po!"

Papa was confused, "Po-po? What is po-po?"

I yelled, "Police!"

Papa paused, shrugged, and resumed picking apples.

Chrissie and I put down our bags of apples, picked

up our machetes, and tip-toed toward where Sarah was standing with Mimi, hiding behind a tree ten feet away from her. The cop walked directly up to Sarah.

"Excuse me, miss," the cop started, unsure of the small shivering girl holding a miniscule shivering dog, "Do you know whose car was parked on the side of the highway here?"

"I sure do, policeman, sir!" Sarah replied, a little too demonically happy for her circumstances, "That is my father's car!"

The cop brows furrowed. "And....where...is your father?

"He is picking apples, sir!"

"What?" The cop started to look scared.

"My father is picking fresh apples so my mother can make fresh apple pie on Thanksgiving!"

"Okay." The cop backed away from Sarah and her demonic smile. He got in his cruiser and left.

Chrissie and I came out from the brush and celebrated Sarah's victory, machetes waving overhead.

"Where did the cop go?" Papa asked, appearing out of the brush with about 57 plastic shopping bags full of apples.

"Sarah got rid of him," Chrissie announced proudly.

"Good. Put the apples in the back and moven-zee!" Papa ordered.

We piled into the car with our free apples, a sense of beating the law, and a new respect for Sarah's cop-evading abilities. On the ride home we were silent over the din of the engine, Mimi's barking, and AM radio, each of us looking forward to some (hopefully) rum-soaked homemade apple pies.

Called a "refreshing voice" by Laughspin, Maria performs nationwide at colleges and festivals and co-produces the Women in Comedy Festival. A Comic in Residence at the Comedy Studio and alumna of Improv Asylum's Mainstage, Maria appears in commercials with Bertucci's, Cadillac, and MA Office of Tourism. She recently hosted an episode of CNNgo for Boston, and ABC's Chronicle, in which a magician, out of thin air, made two red balls appear in her left hand. It blew her mind. Now in Los Angeles, Maria is working toward her dream of starring in a feminine products commercial. **www.mariaciampa.com.**

A Season of Mercy
Teresa Ambord

From the day we brought home our boisterous Boxer puppy, whom we called Mercy, she kept us on our toes. At 8:00 each morning she'd bolt from her bed and go and go and go at full steam all day long. At 8:00 p.m., she'd collapse by my bed and sleep soundly all night. Then she'd do it all again the next day. Her routine seldom varied.

When that first Christmas came, we watched her carefully, wondering if she'd mess with the tree. She didn't. One by one, as presents arrived, we put them under the tree, but Mercy seemed uninterested. We knew some of the gifts were edible: cookies, fancy breads, chocolate candy, dog treats, but she was unimpressed.

We'd had other Boxers, and they had been fascinated by the tree and the presents. They sniffed the tree, pawed at the gifts, broke some bulbs. But Mercy paid no attention. That year we felt very blessed to have a hassle-free holiday season.

Three days before Christmas, we went to bed as usual, and so did Mercy. In the middle of the night a noise woke me. Without turning on any lights, I stumbled to the bedroom door and peeked out. I could not believe my eyes. We'd been robbed! A thief had taken every last one of the presents that had been stacked high under the tree just hours earlier.

How had we slept through this? I wondered. *And why hadn't Mercy barked and alerted us to the intruders?*

I was just about to check to see if Mercy was okay—perhaps the thief had taken my precious dog, too—when something caught my eye. There was a scrap of ribbon on the floor. A few feet away, some glitter sparkled up from the carpet, and farther along, a bit of wrapping paper.

Cautiously I followed the trail, across the living room, up the short stairway into the dining room, past the table, through the laundry room. The trail ended at the doggy door. Not knowing what to expect, I flipped on the porch light, flooding the backyard with illumination. And there was the perp.

Mercy lay under her favorite tree, surrounded by packages of every shape and size, all chewed, pawed, gnawed, and emptied. I guess her self-control only lasted so long. Then in a burst of impulsivity, she had silently, methodically, carried every single package to where she could pillage them in private. Anything that was edible was gone, including chocolates, cookies, bread, candy canes, and four pounds of doggy treats. Boxes lay on their sides, chewed open, left with gaping holes. And Mercy... she just looked guilty and a little sick.

Fortunately nature took its course and Mercy did not need to have her stomach pumped. The next morning we cleaned up the mess in the back yard and salvaged what we could of the gifts. Thanks to Mercy, we had little to open on Christmas morning that year. But the worst part was when it came time to write thank you notes for the gifts we'd received, we had no idea who to thank for what. I know these days many people don't bother to thank people for gifts anyway, but for me, this has always been a point of honor. For the first time ever, I was unable to send heartfelt appreciation of specific gifts we'd received since the cards were chewed beyond readability and the gifts separated from the boxes.

Was that embarrassing? I'd say *mortifying* was a better word. But, most everyone who knows us, knows our beloved dog. Our friends and family had "Mercy" on us when we had no choice but to send out our thank-yous with disclaimers and apologies. To lighten the situation, we took a picture of Mercy looking regretful (this picture was taken after Christmas when the phone rang and Mercy took the opportunity to snatch a donut off my coffee table) and included one shame-faced dog photo with each "Thank you for the ??? note."

We learned our lesson. These days, we keep the Christmas presents under lock and key until Christmas Day. We still can't believe she pulled off her canine caper.

Teresa Ambord is a full-time business writer who works from her home in far northern California. For fun she writes about her family and her pets. Her posse of small dogs inspires her writing and decorates her life. Teresa's personal stories have appeared in several versions of Chicken Soup for the Soul and also several versions of Cup of Comfort and other anthologies.

Twas the Night Before We Killed Santa

Jenn Dlugos

This wasn't the night before Christmas that Clement Clarke Moore promised me.

Oh, sure I was nestled and tucked in my bed, with some sort of sugary hallucinations dancing in my head. But downstairs, creatures were stirring. And clattering. Loudly. By creatures, I mean my parents.

Mom and Dad were elbow-deep in preparations for the feast the next day. Their conversation was poetic, as if they were reciting lyrics to Christmas carols only suitable for Polish families like, *Mary, Have You Heard…the Kielbasa is on Fire* and *No one Saw Three Ships Come Sailing into The Driveway, so Why'd You Make So Much Goddamn Sauerkraut?* This year there were two points of debate. First, Dad couldn't locate the butter tree in the fridge. It's exactly what it sounds like—butter in the shape of a Christmas tree. After Christmas, Mom would buy a dozen of them for 75% off and throw them in the freezer. They appeared on the table for every holiday up until the Fourth of July, because, nothing screams "Go America!" like an ornamental butter bush.

The second point of debate was the Massive Squash. Mom cooked a massive squash for every holiday, but this one deserved its own capitalization. I had never, nor since, seen a squash that rivaled the size of the Hubbard squash we had for this feast. It was bigger than our cocka-poo dog. Hell, it was bigger than most dogs. It probably had its own orbit. The Wiseman should have brought it to Jesus. He would have lived a life of divinity, plus a life of high fiber, as well.

I was told that I would hear upon the roof the prancing and pawing of each little hoof. This was a bald-faced lie. What I heard was grunting. And cursing. And some suspicious hacking. This was followed by a brief scuffle before I heard the distinct, unmistakable sound of a human body being thrown down the cement cellar stairs.

At first, I thought Mom threw Dad down the stairs, because he couldn't find the butter tree. But Mom was never a violent person, even during the stress of the holidays. Plus, I heard Dad talking. I fell down those stairs before. When you do, you lose the ability to speak for a few hours.

Then I remembered a conversation I had with my grandfather. My parents have always been very fond of using their fireplace, especially during Christmas. I asked Grandpa how Santa would get into the house if they had a fire going. He told me that Santa would simply come in through the basement window. This was not comforting, because this was the method of entry used by the hitman in the *Law and Order* episode he was watching at the time. But it made perfect sense in my little kid brain. Unfortunately, it also meant that I knew the identity of the person who was now in a chalk outline at the bottom of my cellar stairs. I marched into the kitchen and asked the question no kid should have to ask.

"Mom, did you kill Santa?"

I did voice my accusation quietly, because our front door was open. We had a bunch of kids in the neighborhood, and they probably had their heads poking out the window expecting Santa to scream, "Merry Christmas to all, and to all a good night." They would be traumatized if they heard my declaration of "Santa, Dead in my Basement" instead.

As it turns out, Mom did not kill Santa. It was the Massive Squash that was thrown down the stairs. Mom and Dad explained that after much grunting, cursing, and hacking it with a knife, they could not break through the Squash Planet's impregnable crust. Therefore, they threw it down the cellar stairs to break it open. They also disputed Grandpa's theory, explaining that Santa was magical and didn't need to crawl through our cellar window like a hitman. I voiced my concern about the temperature in the chimney. Dad said he'd leave a key out for Santa under the big pot on our front porch. This seemed like an ill-conceived plan, as we lived in Buffalo and the pot had been buried under six feet of snow since October.

The rest of the night went as Clement Clarke Moore promised in his famous poem. The moon was on the breast the new fallen snow. The stockings were hung by the chimney with care. And not a creature was stirring. But every Christmas Eve afterwards, right after I left out cookies for Santa, I'd sneak down cellar and made sure that my Grandpa's old Union Carbide hard hat was near the cellar window. Santa might be able to see if I'm naughty or nice, but *no one* ever sees a Massive Squash flying at his head until it's too late.

Jenn Dlugos has won awards for her screenplays, films, and her 1994 Halloween costume. She was recently a finalist in the Lifetime Television Unscripted Development Pipeline. You can find her name on a wide variety of humorous endeavors, including the front cover of this book. If you would like to stalk her from the comfort of your home, you can find her at her humor website **dejennerate.com**, *her screenwriting tips website at* **thescriptscribe.com**, *or on Twitter* **@jenndlugos**.

One Mess of a Christmas with the Family

Christopher Griffin

It was Christmas Eve, the one family gathering each year where all of my maternal relatives are certain to come together. It's a good thing it only happens once a year, too, because that mix of personalities is the recipe for a disaster I would prefer to avoid. The difference that year? After seven months of unemployment, I had finally found myself a great job. I was also dating a great girl. Things had been going so well that a night with my crazy family didn't seem so bad. In fact, upon entering my Aunt Karen's house, it was more reminiscent of the holidays of my childhood than the ones of recent memory.

Almost as soon as we walked into the house, a welcoming committee of children came running over. After hugs, high fives, and introductory handshakes were exchanged, the older kids offered to help take the gifts we brought and place them under the tree. The younger ones stood in front of us, practically blocking us in at the front door. One of them, Brianne, was particularly fascinated by my girlfriend.

"I've never seen you before. Who are you?"
We both laughed at her forward demeanor.

"I'm Susie," she said, smiling at the child.

My four-year-old niece, Isabelle, reached up and pulled at my hand. I leaned over and she gestured for me to pick her up. She cupped my ear and, in a whisper loud enough for the surrounding audience to hear, she asked, "Is that my new aunt?"

I playfully loud-whispered back, "Why? Do you approve?"

With a confused expression, she says "What's 'approve'?" The comedian that she is, my niece was satisfied with the laughs she got, so I put her down, she grabbed my hand, and led us to her parents.

"Susie, right? I'm Cynthia," my sister-in-law introduced herself. "You might be the first date Christopher's ever brought to a family function."

"You might be right, honey," my oldest brother, Ben, said. He then turned to me, "I've got to be honest, little brother, I have been expecting you to come out of the closet every year since you were 12."

If there's one thing that's certain when my siblings and I are in a room, it's that we rib each other until someone crosses a line. Thankfully, when you've been through this time and again for over 25 years, you develop a thick skin.

"You know me, man," I said, "I like to keep my audience guessing."

Sibling banter must be some sort of trigger for maternal instincts because, at that moment, we were interrupted by an excessively bright camera flash.

"That's enough, boys," said my mother, who thinks family gatherings provide the perfect photo-ops to market her stagnant photography career. "Hi. I'm Christopher's mother," she said to Suzie.

They hugged, which was a little weird, though an obvious sign of how nervous Susie was to meet my mother.

"So, what do you do? Christopher hasn't really offered much. I don't even think I got the memo that you were coming."

Susie gave me a playfully questioning look before answering my mother. "I'm a pediatrician."

Everyone within ear's reach was delighted to hear that, though my mother thought the idea of me dating a doctor was absurd.

"A doctor? Are you sure you want to be involved with my son? He's not exactly a model of success, if you know what I mean?"

With a forced smile, Susie said, "I don't think I've ever met anybody with more upside in my life, and that, in my opinion, is the perfect model of success."

She then turned to Ben as we made our way out of the room, "Take my word for it, your 'little brother'? Not gay."

After filling two wine glasses with Cabernet, we escaped to the back porch.

"You're a feisty one," I said to Susie, who smiled.

"I've got to stick up for my man." I laughed, but she continued. "I'm serious. What was all that about, anyway?"

"It's nothing. Complicated family relationships, you know?"

Thankfully, before another layer could be revealed, my Uncle Mitch joined us outside. He grabbed a beer from the cooler.

"So, Christopher, are you working yet?" For the first time since I graduated college, I was able to answer that question without reservation.

"I'm working for a consulting firm downtown."

"That's fantastic," Mitch said.

"Agreed. It's been a long time coming, but I finally have a job that will allow me to take on the real world."

"I hate that show," Susie joked.

Inside, the family had gathered around the dining room table. Karen popped her head out, "You guys should probably come in for this." Her daughter, Sharon, had just arrived.

"I know this is more Christopher's thing, to be fashionably late and all, but I decided to take a page from his book to share this milestone with you," Sharon said, before raising her left hand to show off a notably large diamond. "Jake and I got engaged last weekend. I'm getting married!"

Karen opened a bottle of champagne. "I think this deserves a toast."

As glasses were being poured to celebrate the engagement, my younger brother, Nick, took his glass and tapped it with a spoon. "My wife, Stephanie, and I also have an announcement to share."

Most everybody in the room halted their congratulations to Sharon, questioning Nick's timing.

"Perhaps you all were wondering why my glass is empty," Stephanie said. "We're having a baby!"

As if a tidal shift occurred, everyone's attention turned to the expecting couple. Hugs and congratulations were offered, only to then be interrupted by Sharon, who was incited by my younger brother's attention-grab.

"Really, Nicky? You had to choose this moment— my moment—and make it about you?"

Nick defended their announcement, "We found out last week and couldn't wait to tell everyone."

Refusing to back down, Sharon continued, "Seriously, who announces a pregnancy during the first month?"

Through all of this, I was hoping Susie and I could somehow dodge the drama, but this debate killed any chance of that.

"Isn't it frowned upon for someone to announce they are expecting during the first trimester?" my Aunt Karen asked, directing her question to the only doctor in the room.

"I'd rather not get involved," Susie said, politely.

Apparently, Sharon wasn't satisfied with the response. "Wait, who are you and what are you doing in my house?"

"That's Christopher's new girlfriend," her mother told her.

"Oh. No wonder I didn't recognize her," Sharon commented. "That relationship is sure to last."

That was my cue to interrupt. "Now, I don't want to steal anyone's thunder, but for some reason, now seems like the appropriate time to just come out and say it."

"Called it," said my brother Ben, before enthusiastically giving a celebratory fist pump.

"Still not gay, Ben," I said, "but seriously, you guys make it so easy to look forward to the next time I see you."

Taking Susie's hand, I headed to the door. I grabbed our coats, turned, and made an announcement of my own.

"If any other life-defining moments need to be broadcast, tweet it. Merry Christmas."

After leaving the house, we got in the car, and Susie looked over at me.

"Holy crap, you weren't lying when you said your family is crazy."

I looked back at her, "I'm really sorry you had to see all of that. Thanks for sticking it out with me."

She smiled, and I smiled back. Then, as she started the car, I felt I needed to give her one more warning.

"If you thought that was bad, just wait 'til you meet my dad's family."

Whether creating dialogue and storylines for his action figures at home or drawing and writing about a species of earth-invading alien ice-cream cones in the back of his second grade classroom, Christopher Griffin has always been a natural writer, storyteller, and performer. However, it wasn't until his early 20's, after enrolling in as many writing, film, and pop-culture courses as his college offered, that he realized what he wanted to do for a living. Upon graduating from Emmanuel College with a degree in English & Communications, Christopher found himself a staple of Boston's bar scene, taking on the unenviable role of a 20-something serial dater and working a series of dead-end temp jobs. As one might expect, these experiences provided ample comedic writing material. Finally working full-time, Christopher remains devoted to his craft, spending his time outside of the office studying screenwriting, acting, and filmmaking. If he's not in the office or the classroom, it's a safe bet that Christopher is fixed in front of his television or computer, watching marathons of just about every high-concept program of the 21st Century.

The Christmas That Weighed In

Bambi Marangio

I have three children. Odds are that I will become
a mother-in-law someday. We all learn from our
mother-in-laws. Sometimes, we learn what we
want to become. Other times, well…you be the
judge.

We have been married over 15 years. Ben's mom
never really liked me. This is not my imagination.
When we had our rehearsal dinner, she wore black
and talked to no one. Point served. When
conversations began between us during holiday
gatherings, they were civil and short. She always
had a dagger pointed at me.

Years passed. We have had our share of moments.
My children were growing more beautiful each day.
And smart, too! They won all sorts of awards.
Naturally, it was due to my hubby's side of the
family. I was just their mother, and I guess my
genes and traits didn't matter. One must take it all
in stride and choose your battles. Life is too short.
My husband loves his mother, and I need to keep
peace. Besides, she moved out of state. A few
holidays a year can be tolerated. *Keep positive*, I
told myself. Send cards, gifts, and be nice like my
Mother taught me.

One Christmas, the entire side of Ben's family was
expected to get together. The questions arose,
What to wear? What to bring? What do we do for
the perfect gifts? I shopped with my children. We
really tried to get items personalized and match
everyone's interests. One must be careful,
however. Just because someone drinks, I didn't

want to give them liquor to get drunk on over the holidays. I wanted to be fun, practical, and most of all, liked. It took a full month of shopping to accomplish my task. I was pleased. My husband was pleased. Maybe there will be peace on earth this time around.

We arrived in Texas. No snow like New England, but still a bit chilly and beautiful. It was actually nice to see all Ben's siblings and their children. I always wanted a close family. I wasn't fortunate enough to have that with his side of the family. But this holiday I was going to rectify things, make our situation better, and really be in touch from now on.

Dinner was fantastic. Only two insults in my direction and one question as to why I was still a vegetarian. Our son decided to become vegetarian, as well, but luckily he was not targeted for any discussions. We all laughed, smiled, and listened to Uncle's stories. Strategically, the Lady and I sat at opposite ends of the table. She did the seating arrangements. I didn't mind at all.

Gift time arrived. Kids were excited. I had butterflies in my tummy. I wanted all the gifts to be perfect! As they opened them one by one, all was going well. Everyone seemed really happy and satisfied. My wrapping, intentions, and even the amounts it appeared I spent (appear is the key word here, as I did bargain shop) were all a hit!

Now, this is the moment. The big one. My Mother-in-law brought out a magnificently wrapped gift. The biggest bow you ever did see on top. She placed it at my feet. I wanted to cry tears of joy! Was this for me? A peace offering? I just had our third child a year ago, so maybe she realized that I am a hard-working, loving mother and deserved to be recognized and awarded. I hugged her. Yes, hugged her. Thank you! Thank you! Thank you! Everyone gathered around. I took the bow off and put it on my head. We all laughed. I slowly ripped the wrapping paper, very carefully so not to make a mess and even possibly to keep it. She stared at me, watching my every move. Was she hoping to be as triumphant with her gift giving?

One last flap of the box….and there it was. I stared down at it.

"What is it? Take it out! Show us!" I heard.

I began to shake. A tear fell from my eye. I tried desperately to hold my tears back now. I lifted the gift. My gift. The one wrapped for a Queen. My Mother-in-Law chose wisely, alright. She did put thought into this one. I lifted it out of the box. It was….A SCALE.

No, I didn't want one. No, I didn't need one. I was not attending Weight Watchers or anything like that. I was not even on a diet, but I guess I needed one according to her standards. The room was silent. I finally thanked her quietly and put it back in the box.

I must tell you, that it was totally unexpected. But the scale never returned to my home. That box did, but somehow the scale itself—the gift I will never forget—was under my Mother-in-law's bathroom sink when we left. How did that happen? One will never know. Must have been a Christmas miracle.

Bambi Marangio is a Therapeutic Recreation Director who loves animals and knows the importance of Pet Therapy. She enjoys writing and acting. Recently she has been noted for Just be Julia, a poem about her Mother who has Alzheimer's. Bambi loves her three children and teaches them that as Einstein said, "Improbable does not mean Impossible." Also, she believes that if you make just one person smile and laugh per day, then you made a worthwhile contribution to the world.

It Was the Week Before Christmas and All Through the School...

Kyle Therese Cranston

In one of my past lives within this lifetime I was a 6th grade language arts teacher in a school district not exactly known for its happy and career-fulfilled teachers. The kids were rough (Gangs were a huge problem); the pay sucked (Our paychecks were barely above the poverty level. My student loan officer actually laughed at me when I told him how much I made while begging for a deferment.); and the administration wasn't all that supportive (My current principal was actually pretty cool, but the one I had before him made me cry…a lot.).

Needless to say, it was the worst two years of my life. If you don't believe me or think I'm "exaggerating," check out fellow contributor Alex Freeman's essay. Our schools were in the same district.

Anyway, the year was 2004 and winter break was just days away, which also meant the kids were out of control. I was going through a particularly rough time that holiday season due to a brutally broken heart. I was smitten with a coworker, who had rejected my advances the night before. He had a long-distance girlfriend who constantly bossed him around, which I find odd since she lived a good 600 miles away. To this day I still believe that he felt the same way about me as I did about him, but he was just too scared to leave his controlling girlfriend and take a chance on "us." But, it is what it is, and my life has actually turned out pretty well if I do say so myself.

So, I was sitting at an empty desk in my classroom waiting for my students to arrive. It was around 7:25, and the kids started rolling in at 7:30. I remember staring into space and trying so hard not to cry. I had to get it together because we were actually going on a field trip, and I really needed to be on the ball. Taking 80 6th graders to see *The Nutcracker* was going to require some serious focus and effort on my part. I had to find a way to put my broken-heart mode on pause…at least until I got home and had a bottle of wine within reach.

Suddenly I heard pounding at my trailer door. Yes, I taught in a double wide. It had a spider infestation and was also home to a bunch of other creepy crawlies that I pretended not to see on a daily basis.

My heart stopped when I heard the knocking. It was him! He made a mistake! I was the one he wanted to be with after all! I sped to the door and flung it open only to find myself face-to-face with the mother of a student I got suspended the day before for flashing gang signs in my room. And, she was pissed.

As not-so-stellar as my school was, they were very adamant about halting any gang activity, which meant we were to report any Bloods or Crips talk/hand signals/color wearing right away. Any kid found flashing signs was automatically suspended for 10 days.

She yelled. She cursed. I believe the words "bullshit" and "bitch" were used several times. But, as scary as she was, and she was a scary-looking lady, I felt nothing. No fear. No nervousness. I was so numb from my heartbreak, nothing she said phased me. This probably pissed her off even more.

But, eventually my kids started to arrive, and I couldn't have her berating me in front of them. I worked hard to earn my bitchy, no-nonsense reputation. I wasn't about to let this mad mama squash all the effort I put into seeming "tough." So, I called the principal.

It took him a good 10 minutes to come take her away. My kids watched in horror as she continued to cuss me out. At one point I just looked at the kids and shrugged. *Guys, I got rejected by the guy I'm crazy about last night. This is nothing compared to that. She can yell at me all she wants.* On a positive note, they were genuinely worried about my safety. My students actually liked me! Or at least some of them did.

After what seemed like a year and a half, my principal eventually showed up and carted her off to someplace where she could yell and swear out of earshot of my students' impressionable ears. But, the day was far from over. We had a ballet to attend!

****

Around 9:00 or so came another knock at my trailer door. My students looked up with fear in their eyes as I went to answer it. Once again I shrugged. "Really guys, I highly doubt it could get any worse than that."

I was greeted by another mother, but this time there was no swearing involved. She was Donald from my 2nd period language arts class's mother. I actually liked Donald. He was super quiet and never gave me any attitude. I don't think he sucked his teeth at me once during the entire year. That in itself was a huge feat.

She looked around at my kids and read their apprehension. "Um, I'm supposed to help you chaperone for the trip."

"Come on in. Don't mind them; we had a rough morning," I said as I motioned for her to have a seat at my desk.

"Yeah, Miss Cranston got cursed out!" a few students said unison. "That lady was crazy!"

Her eyes widened.

I nodded. "Too bad you missed it. It was quite the show."

****

We made it to the theater without any major drama, which was rare for a school that had lockdowns at least once a day. I was thankful because honestly given my state of mind, I would've been useless in stopping a fight or worse not losing any kids.

The lights dimmed and one by one the dancers came out. I heard loud giggling coming from behind me. I looked back to see several of my students laughing. *What's so funny? It's the freaking Nutcracker, not Dave Chappelle.*

Donald's mom was sitting in my row trying to figure out why all the kids were laughing so hard.

"You can see his dick!" someone croaked out.

I turned my attention back to the ballerinas on stage and gasped. If you looked hard enough at the male dancers, you could see...um...their manly areas bulging out in their tight costumes.

Donald's mom and I looked at each other, neither of us sure how to address this delicate situation. And then it happened. I morphed in to a 6th grader right there and then as I burst out laughing along with the kids. I mean come on! Male man parts were clearly on display. I was pretty sure Donald's mom lost all respect for me until I saw her mouth quiver as she tried to hold her laughter in, but alas, she couldn't contain herself either. We laughed along with the 6th graders, and honestly, it was probably the first time I had actually cracked a smile in weeks. Yay for balls at the ballet!

Kyle Therese Cranston is a Boston-based freelance writer who is currently focused on trying to bring the word "radical" back into everyday vernacular. She currently writes the Boston Online Dating column for Examiner.com, and her work has also been featured in Chicken Soup for the Soul, the other three Mug of Woe books, and the upcoming compilation The Smoking Section: Memories of America's Most Hated Vice. Besides writing and working on trying to get her first novel published, Kyle likes to spend her time watching Golden Girls reruns, dork dancing, drinking wine, stalking the Travel Channel's Don Wildman via Twitter, and making people laugh with her tales of woe. Want more of Kyle because really, who doesn't? Check out her website: **www.wordswithwit.com***, her hilarious blog:* **nerdrodite.blogspot.com***, and her Examiner column:* **www.examiner.com/online-dating-27-in-boston/kyle-cranston.**

SECTION TWO

Derailing the Party Bus

It's a Wonderful Life
Alex Freeman

I *never-ever-ever* taught hungover. Sure, I boozed excessively each weekend, but on work nights I consumed exactly two glasses of wine; enough to buzz to me to sleep, but not enough to feel anything the next morning. Sober teaching was a struggle and my middle school Special Education students needed my best. No third glass for me.

Fine. I'm lying. I taught hungover *once*. Here's what I remember:

Upon waking, I knew both vodka and wine were to blame. Vodka causes pain between my eyes; wine makes my limbs ache. This morning, I felt as if a leprechaun was lodged inner-cranially and was using a nail to stab between my eyes. My limbs felt as if a sumo wrestler had used them as seat cushions during a transatlantic flight.

I crept to the shower where I soaped my pale, hunched body and hazily recalled the night before.

My roommate Christy and I had hosted a holiday party for our fellow teacher friends. We had taken the party seriously, and although we didn't have a tree, we did have Christmas lights, plastic garland, and a playlist featuring Mariah's "All I Want for Christmas." And alcohol. Lots of alcohol.

The party was classy for a surprising while (in 22-year-old time, approximately four-and-a-half minutes). We chitchatted about vacation plans and sampled Christy's peppermint brownies. Some even discussed their lesson plans for the next day, the last day before Winter Break. I kept secret I had no such plan and intended to "wing it."

Once bored with these banalities, we moved to our true shared interests: alcohol and cigarettes. Shots followed cigarettes and cigarettes preceded drinking games. At one point, standing barefoot atop my couch, I chugged wine from the bottle.

Exiting the shower, I cursed these decisions. Would I survive the day? Calling in sick was not possible; my principal had stated doing so this particular day would require a doctor's note. Scared but resolved, I dressed and crawled to my car.

My next memory finds me slumped in a chair, my head on the desk, the classroom's blinds drawn. The leprechaun was still stabbing, but less frequently; the sumo wrestler's weight lingered, but my limbs were regaining function.

It hit me suddenly: I had nothing to teach. Most mornings, sobriety enabled me to throw together a lesson plan. The seventh grade curriculum was only so challenging. Yet, this morning, I could hardly distinguish between a metaphor and simile. I maniacally searched for my Aunt Patti's *It's a Wonderful Life* VHS.

"Your kids will *love* this movie," Patti had empathetically beamed when lending it to me. Though I had never seen the movie, I believed her in this desperate moment.

The bell rang as I loaded the VHS. The movie would wait until Second Period. First came Homeroom, which required a scripted phonics lesson.

The students rushed in, their loud voices like exploding cannons. I stood, struggling, at the classroom's front.

"What movie we watching?" Tiara asked, smacking her lips and titling her head.

"Hope not some lame piece of crap," she continued, rolling her eyes. Tiara bothered me; she hated absolutely *everything* in the *entire* world. She was the type of person who would call a basket of kittens "dirty, helpless, full-of-shit fuckers." She hated her "trifling" mother and had no friends other than her ever-present pessimism.

Yet, this morning, I sympathized with Tiara. The world was awful. Emboldened by our anger, I furrowed my brow and stared into her eyes.

"We're not watching any movie, Tiara," I responded, opening my phonics curriculum. "We're going to continue with our lesson."

"Oh, hell no. I saw you loading that tape!" Tiara yelled.

"There's a movie?" Anthony asked. Anthony was Tiara's antithesis, perpetually optimistic despite being obese and illiterate. He peered with hopeful eyes.

"Yes, a movie later, Anthony, in Second Period." Anthony, along with a handful of other students, was unluckily placed in both my Homeroom and Second Period. I would not have been opposed to watching the movie in both classes, but after hypothetically watching the movie's beginning in

Homeroom, I would have to rewind at the beginning of Second Period. Thus, Anthony and others would have to hypothetically watch the beginning twice. They rarely paid attention once.

"He gets to watch the movie and I don't?" Tiara spat, the vitriol in her voice increasing my nausea. "Ain't fair." She folded her arms over her chest.

"Tiara, the movie is for Second Period. We have phonics to review. Also, there are students, like Anthony, in both Homeroom and Second Period. They can't watch the movie twice, can they?"

"I don't mind," Anthony yelped. His fat body wiggled in his chair. "I promise, Mr. Freeman. I watch movies two, four, sometimes seventeen times."

"Yeah, we don't care," Angelo, another Homeroom-and-Second-Period student interjected. "Play the movie."

I paused. Any resolve I normally had—not much—was depleted by the hangover.

I stared at Anthony. "You promise you won't complain when I rewind? *Promise*?" Anthony nodded. I looked to Angelo. He nodded. I looked to the other Homeroom-and-Second-Period students. They nodded.

Grumbling, I turned on the VCR and pressed play. I turned on the TV and searched through the channels for the video input. A blue screen lit the room. Tiara loudly sighed, disgusted by my stupidity.

"Anthony," I said, turning, "can you help?"

Anthony strutted to the television, pressed three buttons and made the video work. Several students clapped. While Anthony could never find employment requiring irksome skills, like reading or writing, he might have a future with Comcast.

"I was going to do that," I said, smiling.

"It's broken," Anthony replied, pointing to the screen. "Color ain't working."

"There's nothing wrong with the color, Anthony. This movie was made when all movies were black-and-white."

Tiara went wild. "Black-and-white! You shitting me? I ain't watching no black-and-white bullshit."

"A long time ago like 1970?" Anthony asked, ignoring Tiara, who continued to yell about the unimaginable injustice of the black-and-white movie. Other students joined her.

I cursed my hungover self. Of course they would reject a black-and-white movie. Their cinematic standards ranged from Soulja Boy videos to *Norbit*. Aunt Patti, though well intentioned, had egregiously miscalculated. Ultimately, however, I was the real fool.

Considering the movie was the day's sole plan, the next six hours would be anything but wonderful. I made a mental note to find *Norbit Christmas* next year and concentrated back to Anthony. Perhaps he could learn something.

"In the 1940s, Anthony, all movies were black-and-white."

Anthony's chubby face remained confused. "No color at all?" He was not imagining black-and-white movies, but a black-and-white world.

I laughed. "The *world* had color, just not *movies*. Their cameras couldn't capture color."

Anthony sighed and began to walk to his seat before turning around after a few steps. Approaching me, he motioned he needed to whisper in my ear.

"Your eyes are red, Mr. Freeman," he whispered with genuine concern. Despite my failings, this kid cared about me: a true Christmas miracle. "You been crying?"

I stared my bloodshot eyes into Anthony's. The leprechaun stabbed the nail a few more times. I smiled. "No, Anthony, I haven't been crying," I whispered. "Everything is just fine."

Alex Freeman lives in Boston, Massachusetts. He is currently a graduate student at Tufts University, gloriously sharing an alma mater with his idol, Michelle Kwan. When not stalking Michelle, Alex is completing his debut novel, Schooled, which details his disastrous two-year teaching stint and, should the book miraculously find a publisher, will make him unemployable in any school system. Check out his work at **whatbroughtustothispoint. wordpress.com**.

A Shakespearean Halloween

Holly White

I will never know what gave me the bright idea to go on a Halloween road trip with five kids, my in-laws, and friends who don't actually like my in-laws. We started the trip with three separate vans, no cell phones, and a friend's wife, who was not told the actual distance of the trip because she doesn't like long road trips. Plus there was rain and snow in the forecast. Before we even got on the road, I knew I would have been better off hitchhiking—werewolves, ghouls, and psycho ghost hitchhikers, be damned.

My kids, husband, and I were in one van. Kids really serve no purpose on a car trip other than kicking, yelling, punching, and name calling. After the fifth "I need to go to the bathroom!" (and my fifth offer of a plastic cup), I heard a far more disturbing cry from the backseat.

"Oh my God! Aunt Mary spun out!"

I turned around and sure enough Aunt Mary's van had smashed into a guardrail. There is something you need to know about Mary. She doesn't handle stress well. Her calm state is on par with the Tasmanian Devil from the *Looney Tunes* cartoons.

My husband pulled over and reluctantly volunteered to check on her. My job was to stay in the car with the kids. He muttered at me to watch for passing cars, so he wouldn't get hit. Knowing what was waiting for him, he was probably hoping I'd be too busy watching the kids, and he'd get hit anyway. A trip in the ambulance is almost always preferable to dealing with Taz the Tornado.

Mary's rental van was not OK, but Mary was. Physically, at least. Mentally, not so much. By the time my husband had arrived, Mary had already taken on her role as a maiden in a Shakespearean tragedy. This is why so many characters in Shakespeare's plays kill their family.

There was no room in our van for MacBeth, so she was forced to finish the trip with our friends. I hoped they would still be our friends when this was over.

The woe from this trip should come from the fact that I had to share a small hotel room for several days with my five kids and husband. It did not. It came from the constant hysterical wailing coming from the room next to us to the tune of "I almost died!" MacBeth gave this performance about 20 times, which was heard up and down the halls of the hotel. It was like being at the Stratford Festival. I only wished I could have thrown tomatoes.

We wanted to get in a couple of fun trips for the kids. We found an amusement park that was perfect. Unfortunately, it was on the top of a mountain, and our archaic van laughed at inclines of any nature. It was a long, white-knuckled trip up the mountain, only to reach the top and see a sign that read "Amusement Park Closed for One Week." It wasn't enough that we were the victims of a Shakespearean tragedy, the travel gods also deemed it necessary to teleport us to the Wally World finale of National Lampoon's *Vacation*.

We then tried a haunted hayride for some good

Halloween fun with the adults and kids. MacBeth used it as an opportunity to broadcast her post-traumatic stress disorder to a wider audience. She was convinced—seriously, completely convinced—that the monsters targeted her specifically, because she was in a vulnerable state from nearly sending her car down a ravine. They could see it in her eyes, or something. Quite frankly, I doubted the costumed werewolves along the trail saw much of anything through their latex Party City masks. If they actually could telepathically determine which of us was in a weakened emotional state, we had much bigger problems to deal with, as they were actual werewolves.

The main purpose of the Halloween trip was a hockey tournament for my son. By day four, my husband and I had held five different family meetings to discuss proper behavior on the trip. Not with the children, mind you—with the adults. Specifically, MacBeth.

On our floor were all the hockey families who had been privy to MacBeth's tormented wailings for a few days. It wasn't just the near-death accident any more. MacBeth finds drama in just about anything—a wrong look, laughing, whispering. Even though she didn't talk to anyone, she was convinced the other hockey parents hated her. That might not have been completely inaccurate, given the weird stares I had been getting in the hallways when she cranked up with another impromptu performance. What I really feared was a tantrum. MacBeth invented the temper tantrum. Her fits are a sight to behold: a grown woman jumping up and down with fists clenched, face red, and mouth open, screaming a slur of obscenities. If I could avoid witnessing that, this awful trip would still go down as a "win" in my book.

Going home early was not an option. Thanks to the skills of our son's hockey team, they made it to the playoffs. On top of that, the snow prediction for the next few days was similar to what the Book of Revelations predicts for End Times. Time for another meeting, this time with the only well-behaved people on this trip—my children. My orders were simple: have the vans packed and use the restrooms because we're bolting as soon as the game ends. They agreed. None of us wanted to get stuck in a snowstorm with MacBeth. In her emotional state, she might cannibalize one of us for food.

Our perfect escape plan did not happen because my son landed himself in the E.R. When we emerged four hours later, the End Times had started. The kids worried about getting home for trick-or-treating. I just worried about seeing one of the four horsemen.

Our caravan of three vans began the long drive home. By the first rest stop, the other two vans were missing in action. Even the most incompetent "Walking Dead" characters did better than this during the zombie apocalypse. At the rest stop I learned valuable Mom lessons, such as when you believe your child is potty trained, they probably aren't, and when your child says they're car sick, believe them. Take it from me—it's very hard to wash a child in a public bathroom sink, and paper towels do not make a good substitute for underwear. I also learned that kids' bladders have absolutely no concept of treacherous road conditions. Not even a half hour down the road, my daughter's face contorted to one of distress as she mouthed the words "I have to go." Like a good mom, I handed her a cup.

It took us hours to get home. I entered the house to find my mom, dad and sister, who were babysitting the dogs. Relief warmed over me for just a second, until I heard an all too familiar blood-curdling wail.

MacBeth was standing in my living room jumping up and down in full tantrum. She had gotten back hours ago. In full drama queen fashion, she had called every police station, asking if anyone had found us dead on the side of the road. As if on cue, three cop cars with sirens blaring pulled up to our house. The police didn't really think we were dead—MacBeth had forgotten to hang up the cell phone before her outburst. They overheard her entire tantrum and came rushing over, hoping to stop a Shakespearean family-style murder.

My dogs ran to the seven winds during MacBeth's tantrum. They came out of hiding the next day. I did not. A week passed, and I was still screening phone calls from my in-laws. During this week, I learned my last lesson. Phone calls that come from unknown numbers do not actually mean you don't know the caller. It means the caller is crafty enough to call from an unknown number to get you to pick up the phone. As soon as I answered, I cringed. It was MacBeth, and she had only one simple question for me.

"That was a fun trip! When is the next one?"

Holly will be spending next Easter in a cave on Easter Island, so her in-laws can't find her.

Partying Among the Billions
Denise Robichau

The first point is I'm white. Pinkish, pale
Caucasian, with an unfortunate overtone of
insensitive Western, American, insular, parochial
complexion. A rosacea-prone suburbanite with old
roots back in Ireland.

Curious I am, though, and generally not a follower.
I never understood the childhood chant of "Chinese
School has just begun, no more laughing no more
fun, if I see your teeth or gums, you must pay a
penalty." And, I can use chopsticks. By the
standards of my upbringing, I'm damn worldly and
cosmopolitan.

Still and all, what the hell was I doing buying plane
tickets to truck halfway across the globe in the
Year of the Dog?

In what we roughly remember as Spring 2003, my
not quite husband and I met. (Anniversaries are
better celebrated vaguely without recrimination.)
Not quite husband, because I honestly never know
what to call him, vacillating between the juvenile
"boyfriend" and the sexually ambiguous "partner."
We met, we talked, and we've been talking ever
since.

Putting aside the externals, we have a lot to say to
one another. Politics, religion, books, movies,
people, news, current events, fashion, music, the
1980s, economics, low brow, high brow,
intellectual, and scatological, we got a lot of talking
going on between us. Actually, I should take out
movies. He loves the worst horror schlock made by

man, and that is where I draw the line on compatibility. We also may never see eye to eye on Duran Duran.

You'd never know that we literally grew up in the range of 10,000 miles from each other on a planet that's not quite 25,000 all around. The other side of the world. The side of the world my mother accused me of digging to in piles of sand by the shore. A continent with completely different history, language, food, hairstyles, and a scarcity of potatoes.

After dating for a while and then cohabiting for almost a year, it seemed like a good idea to make the pilgrimage to his ancestral homeland and meet my boyfriend's Chinese family on the island of Penang, Malaysia where he grew up. What I never contemplated, considered, or learned much about was anything at all ever about Chinese people and Chinese New Year. Oh, except I saw Yo Yo Ma perform once.

*****

The first plane landed in Singapore. Maybe if I had known the history of the place, I would have turned back. Your first footfall on exotic lands should never be a converted prisoner of war camp.

We were ragged as we traveled into the future. We lost time to both the international dateline and the numbing boredom and discomfort of 20 hours squashed into economy seats rocketing through the night. Exhausted and hungry, we had our first international fight, sprung from empty stomachs, dehydration, and the despairing disorientation of long haul flights. *Oh boy*, I thought, *I'm about to meet the family of the man who just shouted to*

*the heavens and me that he never wanted a
relationship and it was over.*

The better chunk of another day in the twilight of
Changi Airport we fought, made up, ate a little,
drank as much water as we could, failed to nap,
survived, and jumped on another plane.

I always thought of my family as large. There were
five kids, a mom, a dog, and only one bathroom.
At some holidays, funerals and weddings with
cousins, aunts, uncles, and then a whole new
generation, there was a veritable army of people
sharing some of my DNA. The stereotype is that
Boston Irish Catholic equals a brood.

It didn't prepare me for two carloads of relatives
fetching us from the Penang International Airport.

Getting back to his mother's house, which was
about the same size as my childhood home despite
our second story, it made our celebrations of
Christmases past—at the peak of visiting with wall
to wall relations—look positively Protestant. We
had nothing on this family.

Everything after that was a total blur. I was jet
lagged, worn out, hot as fucking hell. My body had
no idea what day it was and if it were day or night.
On top of that, my erstwhile husband asked me to
manage all of the logistics, and being the white girl
without a lunar New Year tradition that I am, we
either arrived just before the start of the traditional
New Year's Eve dinner or on New Year's Day. It
remains unclear to me, and the family is too polite
to say if the banquet was extra on our behalf or
business as usual.

I remember a lot of people and a lot of food. Eventually, someone offered me a beer, which along with a variety of tropical fruit juices and ice, are necessary for survival on an island hard by the equator with 100-degree heat and about 95-percent humidity. They gave us red packets with gifts of fresh, new currency to herald in a new year of prosperity. We then played cards, and family members quickly won back all of my new bills.

Somewhere in time, as the Year of the Rooster gave way to the Dog, my head nodded and I literally rested my face next to the last bowl of soup at the banquet. I came, I saw, I dozed, a swirl of my new family gambling, talking, and laughing around me.

Leaving roots, family, and some unclaimed junk in New England, Denise Robichau now lives on the coast in the San Francisco Bay area, occasionally turning up at open mikes, comedy showcases, and storytelling events. Her newest form of procrastination from updating her weblog or photo gallery at **http://dee-rob.com** *or working on an unfinished memoir, "Burying My Mom in Leopard Print Undies," is unsuccessfully crab fishing on the local pier or beach while playing games on her iPhone.*

The Thirst of the Fourth
Charlie Hatton

I spent most of the 1990s in Pittsburgh, Pennsylvania. Living in "the 'Burgh" at that time offered a few perks. The cost of living was pretty cheap. Most of the black lung and industrial grime had been cleared away—provided you didn't frequent the South Side bars where smoking had yet to be banned. And they built a nice airport, the better to keep US Air flights from Atlanta to Dallas routing through Steeler country.

But for a guy like me, the very best part of being in Pittsburgh post-1992 was the Pirates. I'd never lived in a city with a Major League team, but here was a doozy. One of baseball's oldest franchises, the Pirates were fantastic in the 1970s, winning two World Series—and then they were mediocre, and then pretty bad, but by the early '90s they were actually pretty good again.

Then I arrived. And they were terrible, and have been ever since.

(I tend to have that effect on things I'm rooting for. Pray you never get on my good side and need to go into the hospital. Trust me, you don't want my "best wishes." It's a kiss of death. Or gross malpractice.)

Of course, cheering for an awful team isn't all bad. For one thing, tickets were easy to come by. Need seats on game day? No problem! Walking up at game time? Pick a section, any section! We could sit just about anywhere we wanted; during one doubleheader, I almost got to coach third base.

63

Well, maybe not "almost." I'm not sure the batboy I was negotiating with had the authority to make that call. Also, we were both pretty drunk.

The relative fan scarcity could be a problem, though. On July 4th, 1995, the Pirates were 14 games out of first place. They were already looking toward next season—or the next millennium—and the fans were, as they say, staying away in droves.

But not us.

My wife and I and a half-dozen friends decided to celebrate Independence Day in the most American way possible—skipping work on a Tuesday afternoon to stuff ourselves with bratwurst, beer, and baseball, then passing out after (or during) the city fireworks spectacular booming just beyond the stadium.

Clearly, this was an all-day affair. The pyrotechnics were scheduled for dusk, the game at 3:00. We hit the parking lot to tailgate a smidge earlier— meaning 10:30 in the morning. We convoyed the cars through the near-vacant lots and picked the perfect spot—facing the river where the fireworks barge would float, not too far from the stadium gate, close (but not too close!) to the nearest set of porta-toilets. We parked in a row and unloaded our supplies.

Much like marshmallow s'mores and military coups, the key to effective group tailgating is planning. If everyone shows up with the same gallon of potato salad or vat of sauerkraut, nobody's going to have a good time. Particularly anyone who happens to be sleeping in the same bedroom that night.

We were better than that, of course. Old tailgating pros, we had schemed in meticulous detail who would bring which goodies, how much, and what kind. Our car was in charge of chips and grill meats—brats, chicken, burgers, and dogs. Car two took care of condiments and side dishes. And the third car rocked the heavy ordinance—two grills, charcoal, plates, and utensils.

And of course, we ALL brought coolers full of beer. Four cases total, give or take a chug. We disembarked and set up shop with all the efficiency and precision of a team of German brain surgeons. Grills, side by side; meats and tongs and sauces on a folding table in between. Lawn chairs arranged around two card tables. Snacks ready in open trunks, coolers on the ground, and a plating/bunning/condiment station stocked and standing by. It was, undoubtedly, a football fan's feng shui wet dream.

We gazed upon our tailgate creation, and we saw that it was good. As the clock struck 11:00 and the grills fired into action, we each grabbed a beer and a chair, saluted 'Murrica and the Fourth, and prepared to toast the occasion.

There was just one teensy little problem. We didn't have a bottle opener. For all our planning—the blueprints, the rehearsals, the emergency contingency handbook—we'd forgotten the opener. And none of the beer was twist-off. And there was nobody else in sight.

The chaos that ensued was fairly predictable. We went through denial first, certain that someone really had an opener and was just playing a joke. A cruel, unnecessary, and unconscionable joke. A few of us were patted down, just to be sure. There was talk of a "rubber glove check." Not a comfortable moment.

Then we devolved into anger. Car three was hardware—how could they not think of this? Car three shot back at us—we were the lead car! The LEAD! Car two suffered a broken tail light at some point; I'm still convinced the dent in our hood was intentional. If we weren't so parched and weak from lack of beer, we'd have been at each others' throats.

Bargaining was next, in the form of "Hey, I bet I can open this bottle with _____." Whatever you might think of to fill in the blank—save "a bottle opener," of course—we tried it. "Another bottle," "a key," "a shoe," "my hand," "my teeth," "Karl," "a hairpin," "this belt," "Karl's teeth"—all of that, and more. And every one a miserable failure. We ruined some innocent fashion accessories, bloodied a couple of hands, and possibly knocked out one of Karl's bicuspids, but we never got a bottle open. As beer-swilling McGyvers, we were utter failures.

That sunk us into depression. Or maybe it was the thirst, or the blood loss. Whatever the cause, we sat sullenly for a while, our monumental plans in frosty cold shambles around us. The grills were hot, but we weren't hungry. The chips, ruffled and crispy, went untouched. Our Fourth of July was in grave danger of going from patriotic to plain pathetic.

That's when one of the guys stood and pointed to the giant parking lot light stanchion a few spots over. He ran over; we followed. He gingerly placed the top of his beer bottle atop the concrete support, the cap just on the edge. Then he kicked it, hard.

The top of one side of the bottle cracked, tiny shards of glass skittering over the concrete. He held the bottle high and with a flick of his thumb flipped the cap off the jagged glass and to the ground. We cheered as though he'd just smacked a Game Seven grand slam. And soon enough, we all had bottles—open, if slightly-to-severely damaged bottles—high in the air, toasting the Fourth of July and our friend and beer and concrete light stanchions everywhere.

We drank a lot of glass that day, I'm sure. And eventually, the crowd gathered around us and we borrowed a bottle opener and probably saved our intestines from further debilitating damage. But the important thing is, we didn't let a little adversity stand in our way. We rose, eventually, like a band of stubborn patriots to realize the American Dream.

In other words, we got shitfaced, watched some baseball, passed out during the fireworks, and all called in sick to work on July 5th. And if that's not what Independence Day is all about, then I don't know what is.

*Charlie Hatton is a Boston-area humorist, blogger and mostly-reformed standup comedian. Charlie enjoys bad-mouthing the designated hitter rule, carrying a bottle opener on his keychain AT ALL TIMES and referring to himself in the third person. He writes anywhere his insolence is tolerated -- like the 'Zolton's Facebook Follies' series on ZuG.com, at Where the Hell Was I? (**www.wherethehellwasi.com**) and right here, in your hand.*

Fright Fest XII: Let it Snow! Let it Snow! Let it Snow!

Kris Earle

October 29, 2011. Fright Fest XII. The day it
snowed on my Halloween party. Yes, that's right.
Snow. In October. In Massachusetts. Snow. Ice.
Damage. New form of terror. Happy Halloween!
Since October 2000, I have held an annual
Halloween party. Each of these Halloween parties
are based around Horror Movies. I select movies in
advance and play them throughout the day. I
normally start at noon and run until after midnight.
In all, I've shown about 100 feature-length and
short films over the past 12 parties and have had
upwards of 300 guests. It's a blast. Everyone who
attends loves it, and I plan to continue scheduling
it as life progresses.

Over the years I have developed a format. Into
each and every Fright Festival I try to get a good
mix of horror from over the past 100 years of
cinema. But in case one fateful day I myself go the
way of the dodo, the movie party needs to live on.
I'm going to let you in on some hosting secrets of
mine. In case you ever want to run your own
Halloween movie party, here are my "Fright Fest"
basics.

For starters, I usually set about 12-14 hours' worth
of entertainment. For those party goers who like to
gab or don't watch movies much, I decorate out a
separate spooky room for them to chat and play
games. Very few guests are die-hard movie buffs.
Most only have the tolerance or attention span to
watch one or two items on the lineup and just

socialize, so I make sure to have a separate, social room. Add candy.

That's step one.

Step two: Pick out the movies!

A classic Universal monster movie is key. *Dracula (1931)* or *Frankenstein (1931)*. Bela Legosi and Boris Karloff were never better and over 80 years later remain icons of the Horror genre.

Pick an "animals gone wild" movie. *Tarantula (1955)* has both a giant spider and a cameo by Mr. "Make My Day" himself, Clint Eastwood (if you blink you may miss it). The *Creepshow (1982)* segment, "They're Creeping Up on You" will make you cringe the next time you see a cockroach.

Pick a weird but scary '70s movie. Something with a floating ball with spikes plus a giant mortician? *Phantasm (1979).* Something with cheesy acting plus fish with razor sharp teeth? *Pirahna (1978).* Pick a television show. A cartoon like, "It's the Great Pumpkin, Charlie Brown (1966)," or "The Simpsons: Treehouse of Horror (1990)." Live action like, "Twilight Zone: Nightmare at 20,000 Feet (1963)." Or "Amazing Stories: Mummy Daddy (1985)."

Pick a film that's truly scary. Something that really makes you squirm. Michael Myers slowly, creepily emerging from the shadows to attack Jamie Lee Curtis' Laurie in *Halloween (1978)*. Little girl Regan levitating her bed, vomiting profusely onto Max Von Sydow's Father Merrin and spinning her head around in *The Exorcist (1973).*

Cult movie. *Black Sheep (2006)* - a genetic experiment makes normally docile sheep become bloodthirsty creatures that terrorize farmers. Peter Jackson's *Dead Alive (1992)* holds the record of most creative ways to dispose of zombies (tip: you'll need a lawnmower). *Evil Dead 2 (1987)* has the best "hero fights his own severed, demonic hand" scene in movie history. Bruce Campbell is amazing in it and is one of the best B-movie horror actors. *Bubba Ho-Tep (2002)* has Bruce playing Elvis and Ossie Davis, a black man, playing JFK as they hunt down a mummy who is killing people in the old folk's home they live at. O.K., so pick two cult movies. Show these later at night when everyone is drunk.

Pick a short film. *Frankenstein (1910)* has the monster with an amazing hairdo. One short film holds the distinction of being shown by me every year since its debut in 2005. *Shake Hands with Danger (1980)*, a short, graphic, cautionary film about the dangers of working with heavy machinery, has been shown seven times now. It's that good.

Pick one newer horror film that came out within the last decade. *28 Days Later (2002), The Ring (2002), The Crazies (2010), The Blair Witch Project (1999), Sleepy Hollow (1999), Drag Me to Hell (2009), and Cabin Fever (2002)* have all made my lineup over the years.

Finally, mix and match as you like. Maybe Hitchcock's *Psycho (1960),* Wes Craven's *Nightmare on Elm Street (1984)*, or a great remake like *The Thing (1982)* or *Invasion of the Body Snatchers (1979).* You can always ask your friends what they think, too!

Step three. Send out your invites.

Postcards if you want to get fancy, email if you don't. For 2012, I plan to make an event page using Facebook and give that a whirl. People will show up, trust me.

"Horror movies, costume party for adults with good food, good friends, and booze? Count me in!"

Invitees show up dressed in Halloween outfits. Past Halloweens we've had Rick as Popeye, Jenn as a Mouseketeer, Eric as Hulk Hogan, Marc and Nicole as a priest and a nun. We've had Mario the Plumber and Seabiscuit. We've had sheiks and Frenchmen shaking hands. We've had wizards before Harry Potter made them famous. We've had Jason Voorhees playing hacky sack with Bob Marley. The Joker and the Marlboro Man smoking cigarettes on the porch. Gypsies and Andy Warhol and Austin Powers. A cow and a hooker. Jesus Christ even stopped by once and offered Wrigley's Spearmint gum to anyone willing to have fresh breath. We had Colin Powell and two Ku Klux Klan members drinking beers together in brown paper bags and laughing (now that was awkward tension). Lenny Kravitz and a lost Asian Tourist. I myself played the role of not only the host, but Princess Amidala, Jean-Luc Picard, the Pillsbury Doughboy, and a Zombie Repairman among others. People come together at these parties. It's a day to relax and have fun, be someone else, and enjoy some entertainment.

Usually.

Fright Fest XII started with a warning. The news. We may have snow. Maybe ice. Maybe a blizzard.

We had all three.

Interestingly enough, the sub-theme I had carried over almost a full year earlier was a snow theme. *Gremlins (1984),* set in December was on the list, along with *Black Christmas* (1974). *Dead Snow* (2009) a movie about Nazi zombies raining havoc in the snowy mountains of Norway was cut, mostly because I couldn't find a copy for less than $25 in time. So icy movies were oddly in the lineup. About 6:00 p.m., during *Gremlins (1984)*, we all started to notice the accumulation. Wow. It's snowing. In October. Not a little, a lot. The porch had a few inches of heavy snow and ice already on it. Wow.

My friend and Woe-editor Jenn made a run for it. She was off to Rhode Island, a two-hour drive, because a horror movie she made was premiering that night. She left her amazing cookies for us and said her farewells.

Little did she know she'd be traveling at 25 m.p.h. the next few hours and would never make it to her appointment. It was one of the worst ice storms in recent history. For the next few hours I would anxiously worry that Jenn had driven off into a ditch on the way home.

The ice and snow were heavy. Since it was October, most all the vegetation still existed. Leaves were still on trees so the added weight of the ice and snow made branches bend and trees creak.

Around 8:30 p.m., in between *Shake Hands with Danger (1980)* and *Black Christmas* (1974), it happened.

The power went.

We had about eight guests left. My brother Kyle, my friend Derek, and I went out onto the porch. It was something similar to a horror movie. It was dark, but you could still see modestly because of the brightness of the snow. Power on all nearby streets was non-existent. Then we heard creaks of things bending. Trees. Big trees. Wind making them sway back and forth. Large amounts of snow and ice falling through branches from time to time. Things snapping. Creaking, snapping, large thuds of snow and ice as it hit the ground. So for the next couple of hours things broke outside. So we went back inside.

I found every candle in the house that we had. Bosenberry, vanilla cream, pine, pumpkin, whatever. They gave us light plus a funky aroma. Plus I found every flashlight I had, including three flashing red emergency lights and three miner-like ICD headlamps to boot.

Then I decided that the party must go on. We must play some charades.

We played charades for the next few hours and had a blast. A lot of laughter inside with some outside frightening sounds for good measure. We thought at any moment a tree would fall on the house and end the party. It was truly a night to remember.

The next day I picked up a giant branch that broke

off a tree. The branch could not have been any healthier and had to be over three inches in diameter. It just couldn't support all the weight of the ice and snow.

Our power was out for eight days, but we survived. National Grid did an awful job getting everyone back up and keeping communication open; it was disgraceful. Over 650,000 households in Massachusetts alone did not have power that weekend and some, like us, were out over a week.

No discounts. No apologies. Halloween was officially cancelled in my neighborhood and many others. I guess that's the true woe of this story. What I learned that night though was as fun as Halloween parties are, there's nothing more real than making the best out of a truly scary situation with friends and family. It was a great night.

In a weird way I'm secretly hoping for something scary for this year's Fright Fest XIII. I have *Alien (1979)* and *The Last Man on Earth (1964)* on the list. Better keep those doors locked.

Kris Earle gives away large Snickers bars to the neighborhood kids on Halloween. He reasons that when they get older and go to egg mailboxes, they'll leave his alone since he gave them the best candy. He also hates candy corn, but when he does eat it, he nibbles each color first away before going on to the next color on the corn. He hosts a show called "Time Travel with Kris Earle" on WMFO 91.5 FM in Medford, MA. Kris has been writing and performing sketch, standup, and improvisational comedy for over 12 years. In college, he once dressed up as a gothic woman on Halloween and no men would talk to him, but he made out with three girls that night. It was awesome.

Revenge of the Leprechauns

Dr. Katherine Howard

I am not sure if I can blame my holiday insanity on
my dysfunctional youth or if it was the result of an
over-abundance of supermom hormones. What I
do know is that when it came time to move from
the house, I had an attic full of Rubbermaid
storage containers full of holiday accoutrements.

The containers were stacked in groups with
permanent ink identifying the holiday within. Eight
containers marked "Christmas," six for
"Halloween," four for "Easter," three for
"Thanksgiving," and one each for "Fourth of July,"
"Valentine's Day," "President's Day," "Martin Luther
King's Day," "Arbor Day," "Flag Day," "New Year's
Eve," "Earth Day," and "Mardi Gras." In the
container marked "Other," I knew I would find the
bejeweled and bedazzled Tooth Fairy boxes I made
for each of my three children. Way in the back of
the attic, hidden behind the old child gate, were
two dusty containers. Written in large black letters
were the three words indicating the once
celebrated holiday. I cringed when I saw these
containers for I knew what memories would be
released should I choose to remove the lids.
Sighing heavily, I pulled the containers marked
"St. Patrick's Day" to the attic door and then
carried them, one by one, down the attic stairs.

A few hours later, when I could no longer put off
the chore if I wanted to have it completed before
the children arrived home from school, I
approached the containers with some trepidation. I
opened the first container and found green
sparkling top hats, various cutouts of four-leaf

clovers, four-leaf clover candy bowls, plastic dishes, and shiny green garland.

As I opened the second container, my palms were sweating. Just under the Irish-themed door wreath was the St. Patrick's Day tablecloth and hand towels. As I moved these out of the box, I saw the tissue wrapped bundles. Lifting one out carefully, I unwrapped the bundle. There in my hand was one of the three Leprechaun Traps I had placed in the container years ago. My mind traveled back in time to that fateful day in March.

It all began in a health food store of all places. I was there on my lunch break to buy some raw almonds for a recipe. At the checkout register, the woman in front of me was chatting with the cashier. She was purchasing some little bags of coin-shaped chocolates wrapped in gold foil. I couldn't help but hear her explaining that they were for the Leprechauns to leave the grandchildren. What a wonderful idea, I thought to myself. I found myself grabbing three bags of chocolate coins to purchase in addition to the raw almonds. I grinned and shrugged to the cashier admitting to having eavesdropped to the previous customer's comments.

In my office that afternoon, I found my thoughts returning again to the gold coins. Exactly how was I going to get the coins to the children from the Leprechauns? Then an idea started forming. The more I thought about it the more detailed it became. I left work early that day and stopped by a local shoe store. I am not sure how many people ask for three empty shoeboxes, but they didn't seem that surprised, and I soon left with the shoeboxes tucked under my arms. My next stop was the grocery store for 8 bags of jelly beans. Then it was a quick stop at the hobby store for some wooden dowels.

I arrived home with the kids and had them busy picking out all the green jellybeans from the many packages while I made dinner. After dinner, the kids painted the shoeboxes green and glued on ribbons, glitter, and plastic jewels. I carefully tied three lengths of thread around three jelly beans. I then tied the other end of the string to an 8 inch length of dowel. The kids and I put the three boxes on top of the St. Patrick's Day tablecloth on the dining room table. Propping up the first decorated shoebox with a dowel, we carefully put the attached the tied jellybean into a small cup and covered it with more jellybeans and placed it under the propped shoebox. This was repeated with the remaining two shoeboxes. The Leprechaun Traps were set!

I explained to my children that Leprechauns would come tonight and they loved green jellybeans. If they tried to take the tied green jellybean, the dowel would be moved and the box would fall down trapping the Leprechaun. In the morning, we would open the traps and the Leprechauns would give the kids gold in exchange for their freedom (don't start in on the moral aspect of kidnapping Leprechauns for ransom; at the time it just seemed like a fun thing to do).

I tucked the kids into bed. I then went back downstairs to spring the traps. I replaced the green jelly beans with the gold-foiled chocolate coins. But I wasn't satisfied with the whole scene. It just seemed too tame. After all, Santa left ashy boot prints, and the Easter Bunny left tuffs of cotton balls when he came and went. A deliciously simple solution bubbled to my holiday-deranged mind. I rummaged in the kitchen cupboards until I found the bottles of food coloring and I selected out the green bottle. Then I went to the playroom and found a small doll that wouldn't be missed.

Carefully dipping the plastic feet in the green food coloring, I created Leprechaun tracks going to and from each shoe box across the plastic tablecloth. Looking at the scene now, it was awesome. The kids would be convinced they indeed caught Leprechauns!

Early the next morning, down the stairs the kids and I crept. We entered the dining room and saw the fallen shoeboxes. Slowly we approached the boxes, and I cautioned the children to stay back as I lifted up the first box. The children squealed with delight at the gold coins laying there. I lifted the other two boxes to the children's delight. It didn't take long for the kids to realize the coins were chocolate, and they giggled as they ate the candy and marveled at the little green footprints.

I basked in the glow of a successful holiday event. Mommy Power was fully charged, and I was totally stoked about this new holiday tradition that I anticipated repeating for many years. Little did I know that trapped Leprechauns, real or imagined, always get their revenge.

During dinner the children asked if we would be setting the traps again that night. I told them no, we only set them once a year. My daughter asked where the Leprechauns lived, and I said I didn't know. They asked how the Leprechauns got into the house; foolishly I replied "by magic." I was tucking the children into bed that night when my daughter voiced concern about Leprechauns wandering around our house after dark. I brushed off her concerns with a casual comment. Then I tucked in the boys.

It hadn't been more than 10 minutes when my daughter let out a bloodcurdling scream. Racing to her room, I found her huddled on her bed looking fearfully around her room. She was crying and claiming to have heard a Leprechaun moving around her room. She wanted to put out green jellybeans, so they wouldn't get mad at her and bite her. Having overheard their older sister, the boys started to cry and wail about Leprechauns coming to get them.

Over the next hour, I repeatedly calmed down the children only to have the night's quiet shattered by their screams as Leprechauns repeatedly tried to catch them. They ended up sleeping in my bed with me that night and the next night and every night for several more months. It wasn't until we sprinkled red glitter around the outside walls of the house that the children were convinced that the Leprechauns wouldn't be entering their bedrooms during the night.

Meanwhile, I had packed up all the St. Patrick's Day decorations. I carefully wrapped the gaudy shoeboxes and the dowels with their string and put them into a Rubbermaid storage container. I marked the boxes and shoved them to the back of the attic where they stayed untouched for years. We never celebrated St. Patrick's Day again at home, except the next year we reapplied the red glitter. Santa never again left footprints, and the

Easter Bunny stopped leaving cotton puffs.

Dr. Katherine M. Howard is a Chicago-based educator and editor who enjoys sharing stories from the edge of parenting (insanity is hereditary; you get it from your children). Once her youngest child is no longer her legal responsibility (and she can claim parental success/survival), she intends to publish a book on the myths and realities of parenting. Dr. Howard's humor has earned her a following and her blogs are enjoyed by many. Following a diagnosis of stomach cancer in December 2009, Dr. Howard uses humorous writing as part of her treatment. Her medical blog can be found at **www.lifeaftergastrectomy. wordpress.com**.

SECTION THREE

Woe the Halls

Christmas Time is Here

Kyle Therese Cranston

Is the wind windier than usual? God, I'm freezing, I thought as I shivered beneath my trendy Gap pea coat. I used to be able to walk around this so-called Windy City in the dead of winter without a problem. I even skipped a hat because I'd rather get pneumonia then mess up my fabulous hairdo.

That particular December afternoon, however, I was bundled up like the Stay-Puft Marshmallow Man. The saddest part of all is that it was actually a mild day for Chicago, too; 30 degrees is considered a nice warm break in the end of December. That morning the Weather Channel even claimed that it was going make it into the mid 40s, making it a warm day, indeed. So, why was I so freaking cold?

Holy big tree, Batman. I craned my neck back like a Pez dispenser, so I could take in the massive tree in its entirety. Ouch. I was a Chicagoan for the first 23 years of my life, and this was the first time I'd ever seen this monstrosity. I looked at the large building to my right, the John Hancock Center. Well, I'd been here before. In fact, I'd eaten way too much food at this Cheesecake Factory on several occasions because sadly in Chicago, that's where you go for a good piece of cheesecake. We definitely have great pizza, no matter what New Yorkers say, but they totally win when it comes to cheesecake. But, I digress. How could I have missed this tree? This called for some serious picture taking.

"Hang on a sec," I said as I stopped abruptly right

in the middle of the busy Michigan Ave sidewalk, causing several pedestrians to glare at me as they were forced to go around my bundled-up frame. I frantically dug into my purse.

"Sorry guys," I said to my aunt and two cousins. "I really want a picture of this."

I fumbled through the wad of gum wrappers, eight billion tubes of Lip Smackers, and various receipts that visually represented the monetary damage of our afternoon shopping adventure at Water Tower Place.

"Dude! Come on," My cousin called as she briskly walked ahead. "I want to hit American Eagle before all the good sale stuff is gone."

But, this was the ultimate Kodak Moment. For one thing, this tree had so many lights on it, I'm surprised it didn't burst into flames. Every inch of it was covered in bright, gaudy red and gold lights. This thing was so bright, I'm sure Stevie Wonder could've seen it. But as gaudy as the tree seemed, it intrigued me. It was Paul Bunyan-sized for crying out loud. It really was quite a magnificent sight.

"Kyle, I can take the picture for you, so you can actually be in it," my aunt volunteered.

"No way!" I wanted to capture this moment, not ruin it with my awkward, bundled-up self. Yes, this essay takes place back when I was Low Self-Esteem Kyle. "It's okay," I croaked out as I tried to get the entire tree in the shot. I wasn't even sure if the picture would come out in the first place because it was getting darker and darker by the second. Yay for Daylight Savings Time! Not!

I pushed the button of my Kodak disposable camera and hoped for the best.

I heard my cousin's giggles through the famous howling Chicago wind. "Kyle, you're totally a tourist!" She laughed so hard she actually snorted. Snorting kind of runs in the family.

"You can't be a tourist in the place you grew up in," my aunt sayed, coming to my defense. She put her arm around my shoulder. "Kyle can take as many pictures as she wants. American Eagle can wait."

"But, it's just a tree? I thought you hated Christmas, anyway?"

I stared up at the massive tree until the red and gold lights bled together. The girl had a point.

I have never been a fan of the holiday season. In fact, I kind of hate everything Christmas stands for: the ritual force feeding that goes on within my family, the being forced to go to Church with my parents and feeling like a poser because it's the only time of year I attend, the grumpy people who fake kindness just for the month of December because they think it will bring them good Karma, and the nonstop playing of atrocious Christmas music. I know I sound like Scrooge McDuck and all, but I guess I've never gotten over the years I spent working in retail during high school and college. My stomach still drops when I think about the countless hours I had to suffer through the cheesy Christmas songs on the suburban Walgreen's radio rotation—my lovely high school place of employment. Imagine listening to *Jingle Bell Rock* over and over again while waiting on old people who must count out their 97 pennies, because they can't bear to break that one dollar bill.

My cousin was right. I did hate Christmas! But, if I hated the holiday season so much, then why did I feel so sappy over a stupid Christmas tree? Yes, it was massive, but where in the world were these nostalgic feelings coming from? When did I turn into such a sap? More importantly when did I become a Chicago tourist instead of a Chicago girl?

I moved away from my south suburban hometown in the summer of 2003. I was fresh out of college and ready to make my mark on the world. More like I was fleeing the memories of the first guy to ever break my heart. Charlotte just happened to have the graduate program I eventually wanted to get into as well as a plethora of teaching jobs. Seriously, you really just need a degree and a pulse to teach in that city. So, I left the only home I'd ever known and drove halfway across the country all by myself.

Big mistake. My body physically rejected the South, and I was so not a fan of anything it had to offer: the heat, the accents, and, yes, even the food. Everything in Charlotte made me miss Chicago more and more every day. I was lonely and homesick as hell. It also didn't help that I was teaching in a school where we had "lockdowns" at least once a day.

The only thing that got me through those first five months until winter vacation was the promise of spending the holidays in good, old Chi-town. I counted down the days until I boarded the plane to O'Hare Airport. I could not wait to let my Grandma fatten me up with her famous Dunkin' cookies. I was even excited to venture out with my mom for some last minute Christmas shopping, even though I knew we would end up spending more time in line than actually picking out the presents. But most of all, I could not wait to just be in and absorb Chicago. I wanted to revel in it. I wanted the crazy wind to knock me down. I wanted my boogers to freeze in the 20-degree air. I wanted to eat pizza everyday or at least until my jeans wouldn't button.

Flash forward three years, and there I stood, all misty-eyed over a lame tradition of a season I loathed in the first place. I looked over at my cousin who labeled me a tourist and knew she was onto something. I was a truly a tourist and no longer a Chicago girl.

But, there was no way in hell I was calling myself a Charlotte girl either. Ew. I made a decent life for myself there, but it really wasn't the place I wanted to hang my hat. Eventually, I would have forge on and find that place, that city, where I can proudly hang my White Sox baseball cap. But in the meantime, I would have to enjoy being a tourist.

Coming Out of the Closet

John J. White

Despite the title, it's not what you think. I'm married, have two children and have no taste in clothes. The closet belonged to my parents and was used once a year to hide Christmas presents from the prying eyes of their five brats.

Although our house in Florida had four bedrooms, it was only 1200 square feet and had nearly a flat roof with no attic, which left only a leaky trunk of a used sedan or my parent's bedroom closet to hide the goods.

I was five when my older siblings informed me Hitler had killed Santa, but I was told not to worry, because Mom and Dad would handle the present giving part of the holiday in his absence. I guess you could say the family was dysfunctional. I fit right in.

Some people recognize their talents early, and by age six there was nothing in that house that could be hidden from me for any length of time. There were four good places for my father to hide his Playboys, and I found them all. This came in handy later as puberty approached.

From ages six to 10, I was inordinately talented in finding ways to defeat my parent's feeble attempt at securing the closet to keep me from finding out what I was getting for Christmas. Even if they were wrapped I could determine by feel, weight, or even smell whether the gift was underwear, a book, or something cool. Toys made overseas had a distinct odor.

They tried everything to keep me out, but 10 years and nine months earlier, my mother never suspected that after a night of bowling, four highballs, six beers, and a misplaced diaphragm, she would conceive a future engineer with an ability for anything mechanical, including breaking into cheap accordion closet doors.

The first year I succeeded, they had tried the greasy James Bond hair across the doors to foil me. The hair was effortlessly found and replaced securely with a little Vitalis from the medicine cabinet, after I had inventoried all my presents first, of course.

The next year the old man pushed the king-sized bed against the doors, easily overcome with the help of two other seven-year-olds in the neighborhood, promised access to old Playboy magazines for their services.

Dad got busy the following year and mounted a hasp and lock across the doors. He wasn't the brightest bulb on the shelf and somehow managed to install the hasp with the four screws exposed. A Phillips screwdriver and five minutes later, I was sorting through tanks, skateboards, and plastic lunar-landing modules.

He caught on when I was nine and mounted the hasp and lock correctly with the four screws covered up and safe from screwdrivers. After careful deliberation, I pried enough wooden slats out of the doors to make room to crawl through to the treasure. When I was through, I replaced the slats so well that to this day they never knew how I got in.

The final time I broke into the Christmas closet I was 10. That year, my father brought out the big guns. The wooden doors were replaced with steel folding beauties securely fastened with a, "by God, Ace Hardware hasp," and a four dollar Master lock in the eyebolt. Tough to crack? Yes. Impossible? Surely you jest.

That year, I really wanted a Gilbert Chemistry Set, complete with 40 chemical-filled bottles, test tubes, and even a small amount of radioisotopes for future nuclear scientists. Safety wasn't a big concern then. And like Ralphie in the movie, *The Christmas Story*, I made sure everyone in my family who worked for a living knew I wanted it.

Faced with the new challenge but armed with a flat head screwdriver, I slid the blade into the spring pins that held the closet on all four sides and it fell to the floor like a rotted sequoia. There, in the back of the closet, behind the new underwear and argyle sweaters, was an unwrapped Gilbert Chemistry Set. My months of whining paid off.

I had the door back up in minutes and was off to brag to my older brother who I was sure was getting the Madras belt and Nehru jacket that was stinking up the other presents.

"I'm getting the chemistry set I asked for," I said.

"How do you know it's for you?"

"Because I asked for it."

"So did I."

"You did not."

"Did too, asshole."

"Did not."

"Did."

"Not."

"Did too."

Okay, now he had effectively thrown some doubt into my head. What if he really had asked for it like he said? I couldn't chance it. If nothing else maybe I could finagle a way to claim part of it. When my mother got off work, I set the plan in motion.

"Mom."

"What? I'm tired, JJ."

"I know. I just wanted to let you know that I think me and Eddie should share any big presents this year, if we get them, anyway."

Her expression didn't change. That was a bad thing.

"You looked in the closet."

"No, really. I'm just saying I think we should share, that's all."

"You *did* look. Okay—fine. Then nothing for you. No chemistry set, no toys, nothing. What do you say about that? You spoiled it for the rest of us. You can think about that in your room."

I came out for dinner, red eyed and quiet. Eddie smirked and my sister chuckled. My two younger brothers still believed in Santa and hadn't heard yet that Hitler killed him, so no one spoke about me and the closet in front of them.

I'd done it now.

Christmas Day came, and I did get presents, but they were all clothes. I knew before I opened them, curse my talent. Eddie made sure I watched him carefully as he organized all 40 chemical bottles alphabetically in *my* Gilbert Chemistry Set. Maybe he'd get radiation poisoning.

I excused myself to go to my room, ready to beat my pillow out of existence. As I was leaving, my sister pointed out the window, smiling.

"Hey, look at that. In the carport."

All of them went to see. My younger brothers both said, "Cool." I shuffled over to see what it was. Through fuzzy tears, I saw a brand new Schwinn Stingray bike with a green glitter banana seat, complete with streamers on the handlebar grips. It had a three-speed gearshift and, I swear to God, slicks.

"Whose bike?" I asked.

"Yours," my mother said. "But you don't deserve it."

I hugged everyone, including Eddie, and then spent the rest of Christmas day riding around the neighborhood, popping wheelies and shifting gears. That night, I parked the bike next to my bottom bunk, one hand tight on the seat brace while I slept.

As I said earlier, that was the final time I broke into the closet to check out my presents. It wasn't worth the risk, and it really was more fun not knowing. And somehow I knew later I might have two children of my own who would have their own inherited ability to find my hidden Playboys.

John J. White has penned five novels and over 200 short stories in the last few years. He has had articles and stories published in several anthologies and magazines including, Wordsmith, The Homestead Review, The Seven Hills Review, and The Grey Sparrow Journal. He won awards and honors from the Alabama Writers Conclave, Writers-Editors International, Maryland Writers Association, Professional Writers of Prescott, and Writer's Digest. He recently finished the novel, Nisei, the story of a Japanese-American teenager from Hawaii caught up in events surrounding the Second World War. He dislikes Brussels sprouts but enjoys writing, surfing (ocean, not web,) golf, and tennis. He lives in Merritt Island, Florida with his understanding wife, Pamela.

The Machine-Washable Messiah

Dave Fox

I almost crashed my car when I saw the billboard.

"He is coming!" the sign proclaimed. Gazing
ominously through the clouds was "Huggy Jesus"—
a crude looking child's doll. I felt like I was in the
middle of a bad *Saturday Night Live* parody. Then
it dawned on me: This was not a joke. Huggy Jesus
is real, and you can purchase him online.

Perhaps I'm missing the point. I was raised in a
complicated religious environment—by a Lutheran
mother and a Jewish father who took me and my
brother to a Unitarian Church on Sundays. Now I'm
a practicing Taoist. It's safe to assume that I relate
to the Higher Power in a different way from the
average purchaser of a Huggy Jesus doll.

So forgive me, friends of Huggy Jesus, if I sound
insensitive. I mean no disrespect. On the contrary,
I'm concerned.

I'm concerned because when I was growing up, I
had three stuffed dogs. Their names were Brown
Dog, White Dog, and Blue Dog. I got them the day
I was born. I took them everywhere. I sang songs
to them and cuddled with them in bed at night.
Brown Dog and White Dog and Blue Dog were with
me always.

"So what's the problem?" you ask. "What's wrong
with little boys and girls keeping Huggy Jesus with
them always?"

The problem is I used to chew on the ears of

Brown Dog and White Dog and Blue Dog. This is what young kids do with stuffed animals. I'm not versed in the finer points of Christianity, but it seems like a not-very-good idea to chew on Jesus's ear.

The Dogs survived other traumas, like grape juice spills. My mother would wash them.

According to the Huggy Jesus website, he, too, is machine washable. But is it okay to put Jesus in the washing machine? Do you go to hell if you get bleach in his eyes?

After my brother Steve was born, we started having stuffed animal fights. I would throw the Dogs at him, and he would retaliate with Kitty and Sammy Seal and Green Froggie. Sometimes, Steve would score a direct hit, and Green Froggie's plastic eye would leave a big red welt on my forehead.

"Steven!" my mother would shout from the kitchen, "Stop throwing Green Froggie at your brother!"

"Dave started it!" Steve would respond as he whacked me on the head with Waldo Walrus. This sibling rivalry is all a normal part of growing up in America. But throw Huggy Jesus into the mix and everything changes. Billy flings his teddy bear at Tommy. Tommy strikes back with Herman the Dinosaur. And in an act of six-year-old desperation, Billy whips out his secret weapon. With Huggy Jesus on his side he can't lose!

His confidence soaring, Billy catapults Huggy Jesus across the room, hitting Tommy square in the eye.

Tommy shrieks in pain, spiritually traumatized. Mom, exhausted from a hard day of being a mom, yells from upstairs, "Boys! Stop throwing Jesus!"

Even as a non-Christian, I am troubled by this scene.

I will admit this: When I woke up, I was in a foul mood. I was angry and depressed for no particular reason. Scowling, I snaked my way through downtown traffic. When I saw the Huggy Jesus billboard, I smiled. Well, actually, I laughed maniacally and almost hit the person in the lane next to me. But the accident was averted, and afterward, I felt happy for the first time all morning. I guess Huggy Jesus works in mysterious ways.

So I went home and checked out the Huggy Jesus website. If you've been reading this, thinking, "I need a Huggy Jesus in my life," here's some important information: Each Huggy Jesus comes with a numbered certificate of authenticity. "Remember," the website explains, "the sooner you order your Huggy Jesus, the lower and more valuable your number will be!"

In other words, you should order Huggy Jesus right away so you can brag, "My Jesus is better than your Jesus."

I guess it was only a matter of time before someone tried to outdo the Beanie Baby. Huggy Jesus is probably a good investment. And who knows? Maybe that low-numbered certificate will score you points in the afterlife.

Yes, the true spirit of Christmas is alive and well,

and the manufacturers of Huggy Jesus will sell it to you for $29.95 plus seven dollars shipping and handling.

Just please, keep Huggy Jesus away from the family dog.

Dave Fox is a freelance writer based in Singapore. He has written two bestselling travel books: Getting Lost: Mishaps of an Accidental Nomad, *and* Globejotting: How to Write Extraordinary Travel Journals (and still have time to enjoy your trip!) *He also teaches online travel and humor writing courses and offers one-on-one writing and humor coaching. For more information, please visit his website at* **globejotting.com***.*

Zombies Alive!
Teresa Roberts Logan

Halloween is my favorite holiday. No contest. And not just because I love zombie movies. *Shaun of the Dead. Night of the Living Dead. Dawn of the Dead* . . . aaaah, the warm, fuzzy classics. Now add to that list of screen zombie love: *Zombieland* and *The Walking Dead*!

There is something so visceral (ha!) and basic about the struggle for survival in these flicks, people running to escape from the never-ending wave of slow-moving zombies. The zombies never run, though, they slog. Somehow, the zombies actually even catch some of the running people.

Yes, in running from zombies, you don't have to juggle your priorities, you pretty much know. To-Do List: Flee.

With everything you have, flee the undead. Hey, there's a bumper sticker! "Flee the Undead." A good thing to remember during election time. I'm copyrighting this as we speak.

Some people don't find zombies scary because zombies are...slow. Probably because they avoid energy drinks. But they keep on coming. This is very scary to clumsy people. Like me. Because you know that moment in every scary movie where somebody trips. They are goners. You can pick these people out from the beginning. We take bets. "10-to-1 the accountant gets it in the first half hour." Wholesome fun. That's what I'm all about.

Zombies seem to, despite their apparent lack of

focus and devil-may-care fashion sense, have a very admirable, desirable quality: persistence. We should all be so driven.

And, when the world economy is tanking, people are regularly yelling ugly ignorant things at election rallies and gas prices are jumping around like erratic little jumping beans, it's deeply comforting to know that someone, somewhere, is just fighting to keep their brains from being eaten.

I mean, now, that is getting down to brass tacks.

I worked on a zombie movie in college, called *I Was a Zombie for the FBI*. I was in seven scenes and was Assistant Art Director. It's now in "Cult Classics" on Netflix.*

I think the main reason they let me work on the movie, though, was because my mom worked for a meat-packing company, and I could get free pig guts for us. Yes, that's what I said. Pig guts! Free! Because there are some things in life you just shouldn't have to pay for. Parking is one. Pig guts are another.

To truly appreciate the magnitude of what I gave personally to this film, you have to know that I am "practically a vegetarian," according to my mom. And you must also understand what a weak stomach I have. Seriously. Sometimes I declare a moratorium in our home on episodes of CSI. We have a house rule that no one can make vomit noises. Not even if they are actually vomiting.

Yep, I was carrying around a cooler full of pig guts. How to win friends and influence people, indeed.

So, nowadays when I get discouraged or distracted by life's little tricks and twists or election cycles that last a millennium, I pull out a good ol' zombie movie. It focuses me on what's really important.

And all is right with the world again.

*The other day I was in a video store, one of the old-fashioned kinds which still carry VHS tapes, and I found our movie! There it was, *I Was a Zombie for the FBI*! It was in a section they had entitled: "Tasteless." Yes, I've suffered for my art.

Teresa Roberts Logan, sometimes known as t.r. logan, is a comic and cartoonist and art teacher, oh my! She is also a night person, who feels like a zombie daily, until about 11 a.m. Her website is **www.LaughingRedhead.com***, and her blog site is* **www.LaughingRedhead.me.** *Her book of cartoons, "The Older I Get, The Less I Care" can be purchased at* **www.Amazon.com.**

Trees That Capture the Spirit of the Season

Bill Thorndike

Yes, Virginia fully-trimmed Christmas trees sometimes crash to the floor in an explosion of sparks and tinsel and shattering glass. This is not just the stuff of Hollywood. As a child, I witnessed such a spectacle. I may have caused it. I was certainly an accomplice, if not the actual triggerman.

In those days, we usually bought our Christmas trees after hours in parking lots illuminated by a single string of light bulbs. The vendors were tired-looking fellows. They wore big parkas and had whiskey on their breath. Back then, the idea of going to a tree farm and cutting a live tree would have seemed quaint, like something out of Currier & Ives.

But almost everyone in the neighborhood had a real tree. Christmas wasn't Christmas without the smell of balsam. The Ljunquists across the street always had huge trees that ended abruptly at their seven-foot living room ceiling. They were decorated with candles and simple homemade stars and angels. In the evening, Mr. Ljunquist would play carols on his accordion. Mixed with the sweet aroma of his wife's hot-cross buns baking in the kitchen, you might as well have been in Sweden.

There were a few exceptions to the real tree rule. My friend Chris lived on the avenue in an upstairs apartment. His family had an artificial tree. It was the kind you would sometimes see in the windows of auto dealerships, those sparkling metallic numbers that went from blue to green to red and smelled of plastic and cigar smoke.

One year Chris got a bow-and-arrow set from Santa. This was in the days before such gifts were considered either insensitive or life-threatening. He and I decided the star that topped his silver Christmas tree would make an ideal target.

It is here that my memory becomes a bit clouded. Either Chris took aim or I did. The result was that his shimmering, orb-laden tree began to move. At first, the movement was barely perceptible. Then, as if in slow-motion, that great artificial sequoia made its steady descent, landing in a magnificent crash of shattered glass and broken colored lights.

Seconds later we could hear Chris's mother screaming at us through uncontrollable sobs as we made our escape down the back stairway.

This year we've heard and read much about whether Christmas trees should properly be called Christmas trees. If ever a Christmas tree was not a Christmas tree, it was that fallen mass of mangled plastic and broken glass.

Yet, in keeping with the season, a miracle took place. Two miracles, actually. After a couple of days, I was forgiven and allowed back into Chris's house. When I reentered the living room, there stood the silver Christmas tree, as though nothing had happened. With lights on and most of the ornaments replaced, it was a festive sight to behold.

We got our tree this past weekend. Years ago we would have gone up to Wesolowski's on Lantern Hill Road. We used to find Jim in his shed, hanging out by the woodstove. We'd talk for a while, then he would hand us a saw and we'd get lost in his long rows of overgrown pines.

Those days are gone. We went to another local farm this year. It was very efficient and well-managed, although waiting as we did until a week before Christmas, we noticed most of the better trees had been tagged. My wife, who is not a tall person, picked a tree about her height. It stood by itself, unclaimed, within shouting distance of the car.

"Here," she said.

"But there are more out there," I said, pointing across the field. "Bigger ones."

"Here," she repeated. Her feet were getting cold. "This one's good."

We brought it home and set it in a stand. It had about two feet of air space to spare, enough room for a band of angels, a whole constellation of stars.

It is a sweet little tree.

Bill Thorndike and his wife, Marthee, live in an old house in Mystic, CT. He has two adult children, and he and Marthee have a 1st grader and twins in pre-K. He has been compared to Father Time. In 1992, Bill and several friends started a local newspaper, the Mystic River Press. That same year he started a novel, which he plans to publish in 2026, after the twins are out of high school. "The novel will explain everything," he said.

Once Upon a Last-Minute Christmas

Scott Sevener

The year was 2006.

In fact, it was the first year that I'd spend Christmas together with the girl who would eventually become my wife. In hindsight, that should have motivated me to get some amazing presents under the tree in a timely manner, but as they say, lazy habits die hard.

I don't remember the exact distraction at the time—maybe I was a bit pre-occupied by the latest video game to grace my Playstation 2, or maybe I was just too busy watching episodes of *The Office* back in the day when the show was actually funny to want to leave the comforts of my own home and venture out into the general craziness that is the world of holiday shopping. I mean, for what it's worth, I don't exactly blame myself for that. Shopping during this time of year most certainly is crazy, from the insane crowds at the mall to the even more insane crowds outside in the parking lot. When they get behind the wheel, you can see from the look in their eyes that they'll stop at nothing—actual stop signs included—to get to that next sale while the Zhu Zhu Pets are still hot!

If you ask me, you'd have to be crazy not to want to avoid all of that candy-cane-induced chaos as long as humanly possible. Of course, since Christmas does unfortunately come but once a year, eventually there comes a time when a guy has to suck it up and get with the spirit of the season if he wants to avoid re-gifting old magazines and canned corn to the girl that he's actually hoping will stick around at least through the foreseeable future.

For me, that time came right around 6:30 p.m. the night of Christmas Eve.

And as you might expect, this is where our story gets interesting. As most retail workers will profess joyously in relief, 6:30 p.m. on Christmas Eve is the time when the vast majority of stores have finally called it good and closed up shop until after Christmas, leaving an increasingly dwindling number of options for stragglers like myself.

Aside from 7/11 and maybe ABC Liquor, neither of which was going to be particularly great for my relationship, my options were hovering weakly between slim and none, and at this point it was going to take some quick thinking to get myself out of this Christmas Eve kerfuffle.

Like Mrs. Claus preparing breakfast for a hungry group of elves, I was going to have to scramble. Fortunately, living here in Central Florida, as I tend to gloat about to my frigid brethren of the North from time to time, I did have one alternative resource at my disposal that was admittedly a bit unorthodox. However, as desperate times call for desperate measures, it was with panicked haste that I grabbed my shopping list and pointed the car towards the one place in Florida that was guaranteed to still be open for business at 6:30 p.m. on Christmas Eve…Disney World.

This wasn't the first time that Mickey Mouse managed to come to my rescue. Considering that the following spring I would return to propose to that very same girlfriend with the help of a few of his friends, it certainly wouldn't be the last, either. I suppose in retrospect it just made sense that of the few places left for last-minute Christmas shopping, the most popular tourist destination in the country would still be alive and kicking in the final hours before Christmas itself.

And kickin', it most certainly was! Stores elsewhere were locked up tight, their parking lots long since deserted, but the streets of Downtown Disney were bright and bustling with tourists partaking in all of the festivities that Disney has to offer, from live music and dancing in the streets to snacking on all sorts of holiday treats to even some last-minute photo opportunities with the big S. Claus himself.

Granted, I had my own last-minute activities to partake in, so sidestepping all of the other merry fun as best I could, I slipped in and out of the massive crowds like a shadow in the brightly illuminated night, a man on a mission to save Christmas!

Some Mickey Mouse socks, a Pirates of the Caribbean beach towel, an Eeyore mug that depicted the tragedy of mornings without coffee—if my girlfriend hadn't already been tested to see just exactly how much Disney she could tolerate in her life, Christmas morning was going to be it! Actually, it was surprisingly easy to find a variety of gifts that weren't entirely Disney-related during my 11th hour shopping quest, and by the time the clock struck midnight and even the Disney shops were getting ready to send patrons back to their hotels for the night, I was back in my car with a trunk load of goodies racing home to get them all wrapped and under the tree before my night-shift-working lady friend would return home in only a few hours.

It was indeed a race against the clock until the very end, but when morning came and all of those last-minute presents were ripped open just as happily as any, I knew that my holiday cheer had persevered once again.

Good, old-fashioned lazy holiday cheer.

Scott Sevener is a humor columnist who enjoys writing funny narratives about the random things in life that amuse him. His first book, a collection of humor columns entitled The First Seven Years Are Always the Hardest... is available now at **comedic-genius.com**.

The Halloween That Lingered

Renata Roskopf

We were 13 and best friends. We wanted what all girls that age wanted, to be older. We found ourselves with less adult supervision, doled out in valuable chunks of time. We knew "a mind [was] a terrible thing to waste," and so were these opportunities. Lucky for us, too, it was Halloween. We were young enough to trick-or-treat and still on the cusp of discovering what older kids did on this holiday.

We heard stories about eggs that might make the Easter Bunny retire, or even, lay himself off. That Halloween, despite that food was sometimes lacking, we were learning the beauty of choice. My own mother made me eat left-over hard-boiled Easter eggs, long past the holiday, even with red and blue paints soaked through. "It's food coloring! I don't care if the egg is purple inside. It's still good. Eat it!" But now, we could sneak eggs from Samantha's refrigerator, carry them with us, and maybe even throw them. Somewhere.

We did our makeup. Samantha's eyes were grey globes, and they'd crust after applying her newly acquired skills, drawing thick blue tracks of eyeliner on both lids. Tonight was no different, except we had on more makeup and enough rubber Madonna bracelets on our arms to increase our chances of a safe bounce from a hit and run, plus we aerosoled our hair neon pink, which made us choke a little. It didn't matter what we were, all could have pink hair!

Missy, Sam's little sister, got ready, too. She was

an 11-year-old, short, blond-and-pink-polka-dot-haired Raggedy-Anne. I sewed an Arabian Knight costume from pieces of white flannel and gold lame, while safety-pinning the difficult areas, like the waist. Samantha was a witch because her mother would dress like one when going to a bar for Halloween. It was a grown-up costume, Sam thought.

After a couple hours of door-to-door, and we were satisfied with our collections, we walked by my old middle school, The Washington Irving. It brought back memories of sixth grade. Sam and I met in the seventh grade at Latin School as "sixies," because we had six more years to graduate. The countdown was on. Sixth grade seemed like more than a year ago. At the Irving, I remembered fending off invitations to fight, "Dee," aka Demetrice, in the bathroom at lunch. About five girls stood by the door waiting, so I'd slip out of the lunch line, down the side stairwell to the cafeteria instead. Most everyone did what these girls wanted, even some boys. One day after school, our homeroom teacher wasn't in class. My attempts to avoid fighting Dee ran out. Homeroom became their bathroom, except with a bigger audience, the entire class.

After Dee pulled me to the floor by my hair, I struggled to stand. Then, I did what any sixth-grader who wanted to avoid further pain would do. I started punching Dee away from me and restraining her. Suddenly, Dee's friend LaShonga, the leader of the group, cheered me on. Even though the roots of my hair were bloodied and scratches covered my face and arms, to her, apparently, I looked like some sort of winner. "You're my daughter" LaShonga said, despite her being one-year older than me at most. This was her seal of approval. I didn't have to defend myself or avoid the bathroom the rest of that year. I was confused, and lucky.

That Halloween night though, our concern was the older kids drinking in the school yard. If we threw an egg, what would they do? But we didn't see anyone. Memories of the fight somersaulted between thoughts of slamming eggs at the school. I didn't want to fight that girl. I didn't want her to lose a fight, and I certainly didn't either. I didn't want a fight period.

"I dare you to throw an egg," Sam said.

"Really?" as if I could with one more reason.

"Well, if you don't, I will." she said, and after walking back and forth a few times, she threw one, and I threw mine right after, like catapults. Splat. Splat. The doors appeared further away in the darkness that hung in the air. Truth was, we were probably too afraid to throw them at someone's house. A closed school seemed safe. Plus, the fights seemed to justify it.

"I want to throw mine!" Missy's face was red, even well beyond her drawn-on cheeks. It was cold out. A tear almost popped out of her eye, as if forecasting that this too, would be something she would miss out on, because she was younger.

"We can't; we have to get outta here!" Samantha said, and dug her high heels into the sidewalk to walk faster. Reluctant, Missy followed, afraid she might not find her way home. Really, we walked way too far.

Finally, when we came to the street that ran along the woods and tracks, just off of Hyde Park Ave., we lit Old Gold's Sam sneaked from Paul, her mom's new boyfriend. We didn't like Paul, but we decided to give his cigarettes a chance. We inhaled slowly, not realizing how unfiltered cigarettes pull your insides out.

"I'm gonna tell on you guys!" Missy threatened, after we denied her pleas to try one.

Then a car drove by, full of teenagers. Missy blurted a proud, "I threw it!" as her previously neglected egg flew over a telephone wire to where we couldn't see. And we ran. Sam couldn't keep up, wearing high heels, despite our plan to scale most of Hyde Park and Roslindale that night. The car stopped. Two kids got out and ran toward us. Missy and I kept running until the car's thudding exhaust kicked back up and dissipated with rear lights into the blackness.

Samantha's face was slimy; worse than beauty tricks we tried from Sassy Magazine.

"You alright?" I asked. Missy popped out with "Ghostbusters!" and "You've been slimed," and chuckled, hoping humor would deflect Sam's irritation, but Samantha's face was concrete, underneath dripping egg.

"Shut! Up!" Sam pushed Missy. Missy's whole face squeezed back tears. She didn't bother to snap back at Sam. Instead she was happy she threw her egg, and Sam paid for it in seniority, and her decision to wear heels that night. We all walked the block back to their house, where no one was home, and we got ready for school the next day.

A month later, we drove by the Irving in some adult's car. I forget whose. But dark stains from the splattered eggs lingered on the green entrance doors. And we laughed, sharing our secret little victory. Months later, we walked by, still there. A year later? Yes. Dark green spots on the door, through rain, snow and an entire summer beating sunlight, proved the prior Halloween had turned all three of us into some type of werewolves who throw eggs. Sometimes, I wondered if I could wash it off, but the stain had to be twenty-feet high. I'd need special supplies. I'd need a car. I'd need to be at least sixteen to drive, as old as the teens drinking in the schoolyard on weekends.

Renata Roskopf grew up in Boston. She has worked from the age of fourteen and was lucky to have many different work experiences since. She studied English and Economics at UMass Boston, studied abroad twice and graduated from Boston University School of Law. She wrote poetry in college and was published in The Watermark and The Boston Poet. More recently, she read at La Luna and Out of the Blue in Cambridge. Her current focus is on prose and storytelling. Education and children's issues have been a longstanding interest and focus of her writing.

SECTION FOUR

Cupid Missed

Excuse Me While I Kiss This Guy
Jennifer Worick

Once upon a time, I dreamt of Prince Charming and true love's kiss. Three months into a relationship with Aaron, I thought my happily ever after had come at last. Not so much. My fairytale romance didn't start with a kiss, but on a certain New Year's Eve, it sure as hell ended with one.

Old acquaintance should not be forgot, but most of my New Year's Eves should be kicked to memory's curb. December 31 has, to put it mildly, *not* been kind. Not for a long time, and not by a long shot. December 31, 1990 found me in Detroit Receiving Hospitals ER with an exposed patella and a ruined Ann Taylor skirt. This was an improvement on things, seeing as the year before I was heartbroken, wandering around a party on the other side of the country sporting a party hat (not a euphemism) and carrying a 12-pack, only to bump into my ex with my replacement on his arm. This scenario has been par for the course, so I don't know what I was thinking when I ventured out with my new squeeze Aaron and a group of friends to a dive bar shortly after ringing in the New Year. I should have left well enough alone and not poked this particular bear. I didn't see it then, my vision obscured by champagne-colored glasses, but the night had disaster written all over it.

In my defense, there was no warning save my history with the holiday. I was sipping on a gin & tonic, chatting up a few tipsy strangers when all of the sudden, everything went David Lynch—like full-on batshit *Twin Peaks* meets Dennis Hopper-in-a-gas-mask David Lynch. In slow motion, I watched as Aaron sidled up to the guy I was talking to, hooked his index finger into the waistband of his skinny hipster jeans, pulled him towards him, and kissed him on the mouth.

At this moment, I would not have been at all surprised to see a dwarf in a velvet suit dance by.

Mouth agape, I stood frozen, mortified, humiliated, did I mention frozen as my best friend jerked her finger in their direction, asking, "Did you see that?" I shut my mouth, put down my gin & tonic, grabbed her hand, and walked out. Prince Alarming called 15 minutes later, wondering where I was and telling me he was going to smoke some weed with his new make-out buddy and friends. When I added "white-hot pissed" to my initial response, I left him a measured teeth-clenched voicemail explaining why I fled the scene. I received a reply after a week, a vague four-sentence e-mail that read like a form letter. In all my dreams, fantasies, and projections, never did I imagine that my prince would blow me off via a Hotmail account.

Before New Year's Eve, I had been thinking that things with Aaron were moving too fast. I thought I was the one who was serving up commitment-phobe, who was screwed up. Well, in the words of musical genius Richard Marx, "I shoulda known better."

I should have known better than to date yet another Cancer and not branch out into other signs of the zodiac. I should have known that a 32-year-old divorced man with a penchant for PBR—lots of PBR—doesn't want a girlfriend breaking his stride. I should have known not to care so much early on. Well, I didn't know better and got smacked down on New Year's Eve, which, come to think of it, I should have known to avoid.

But I'm learning. I've also learned a few other things about myself. For instance, I never knew where I drew the line of dating bisexuals and/or alcoholics and/or asshats. I never knew just how much care and respect I require from a date. So thanks, Aaron, for providing me with heightened self-awareness, even if you are hopelessly confused.

While I've polled men and women on the subject and they all agree that straight men do not kiss other men on the lips—ever—it really doesn't matter if they validate my actions or feelings. Based on the emotional gut bomb that exploded in my belly that night, I now know what two of my deal-breakers are. I may not require a fat wallet or marquee looks, but I do require consideration and heterosexuality in my date. He didn't even have the manners to say—to paraphrase Jimi Hendrix's "Purple Haze"—"Excuse me while I kiss this guy."

So I'm going to back to my wish list and doing a bit of tinkering: whipsmart, kind, thinks I'm the bee's knees, doesn't kiss men (or anyone else) in front of (or behind) me… The list goes on and alas, so does my search for a prince of a guy. But I'm cheered by the notion of all the new frogs—er, men—I get to kiss. And, come to think of it, maybe Aaron's thinking the same thing.

Named one of the four funniest bloggers in America by Reader's Digest, Jennifer Worick is the New York Times-bestselling author of more than 25 books, including Things I Want to Punch in the Face and The Prairie Girl's Guide to Life and, perhaps appropriately, The Worst-Case Scenario Survival Handbook: Dating & Sex. In addition, she is a blogger, publishing consultant, and public speaker. She lives in Seattle.

Infamous Birthday
Sarah Blodgett

It was December 7th, 2000, 59 years after the attack on Pearl Harbor, and the only person more excited than me about my 21st birthday was my best friend Ricki. Ricki had turned 21 five months earlier, but since I was really her only friend, she couldn't celebrate until my birthday. We had been friends since junior high, but we didn't have much in common. We were really just friends out of convenience at this point.

Ricki had met this guy a week earlier. I think. I'm still fuzzy on the details, because she was always finding men somewhere, but I think they met at a gas station.

"He's kinda cute; he has a car, and he has a friend," she told me.

I was skeptical.

The night of my birthday Ricki came to the door and pulled me onto the front porch.

"I'm so sorry, but your guy's not very cute, don't be mad."

Ricki gets in the back seat of the SUV parked in front of my house, so I slid in next to her. The guys turn around and say hi. They may have told me their names, but I was too distracted. They were 40-something Arab men that barely spoke English. One was bald with a "Mr. Clean on acid look," and the other had a full head of hair that sat like a bouffant on his head and was wearing a Bill Cosby sweater. I should have ran back in the house but panic set in.

We went to the El Morocco, a nightclub in my hometown that doesn't still exist, and for good reason. The club was split up into two rooms, a dance club and a bar. We went into the dance club and found a small table in the corner. We ordered drinks. I ordered a Pearl Harbor because my birthday was Pearl Harbor day, and I thought it was a cute thing to do. Plus, I needed some way to amuse myself. Bouffant was sitting next to me, and he kept sitting closer and closer. I guess he was mine.

 "Ricki, we need to go to the bathroom, NOW," I said loudly.

We stepped into the crowded bathroom. "I'm leaving; I'm calling my parents to come pick me up," I yelled. People were staring but I didn't care.

"But we can't ditch them; they paid for us to get in. We owe them," she said as if it was her moral duty.

"It was $5; I will give them $5." I wanted to prove that I could not be so easily sold into white slavery.

"We can just go hang in the other room for a while to get a break from them," she said trying to calm me down.

We sat at the other bar and ordered another round. Then Ricki decided we should do shots of Hennessy because she had heard it was something that people took shots of. We ordered two shots of

Hennessey and got two snifter glasses with about six shots worth in each glass. We chugged them. We were drunk. We were also caught. Bouffant and Mr. Clean had spotted us and they were angry.

"Get your coats, we're taking you home."

They yelled at us the whole way home. When we got to my house, I jumped out of the car and ran in assuming Ricki was behind me. My parents came running to the door asking what was wrong. Trying to hide my intoxication I asked why they thought something would be wrong.

"Because," my mom said, "you have only been gone an hour."

"It was the worst night ever," I said plopping on the couch. My mother was spying out the window.

"The guys were terrible, old, and creepy," I said.

"Were they really that bad?" my mother asked.

"Yes," I said firmly.

"Then why is Ricki making out with one of them on the front lawn?"

Apparently this day would live infamy.

Sarah Blodgett is comedy's Funny Honey. Sarah's work has been featured in The Comedians magazine, Reader's Digest, and the original Mug of Woe. This Funny Honey also performs stand-up comedy throughout the US. Check her out at **http://www.funnyhoneycomedy.com/**

Just Watch the Fireworks

Christopher Griffin

It was the summer of 2009 when I met her. We had been dating for nearly two months when she asked if I wanted to be exclusive. I was still getting over a relationship that ended the previous summer, and the idea of having a "summer girlfriend" to enjoy the season with seemed appealing. Plus, I was interested in seeing where it would go, so my response to her was, "Sure. Why not?"

I assumed exclusivity meant that we would continue doing what we had been doing, only without concern that one of us would meet someone else as we got to know each other. I never thought that "being exclusive" would mean enduring one of the most uncomfortable moments of my dating life.

"I'm really glad you decided to come. Everybody's going to love you," she said to me.

We were heading several towns over for a Fourth of July barbeque at her best friend's house. Hey, I'm all for meeting new people. Besides, it was scorching out, so it would be nice to take a dive in their pool. I looked forward to eating good food and enjoying the weather and the day.

"The view from her place is perfect for the fireworks once it gets dark. It's going to be great," she continued.

All was well until we pulled in to the driveway when, patriotism and the always welcome smell of a fired-up grille notwithstanding, I hoped we had the wrong address. Of those present in the yard, there were only four others who fell into the 20-30 age bracket, of which I was comfortably in the middle. Never mind that as soon as I stepped out of the car, I was being introduced as "my new boyfriend" to a group of individuals named "Mom," "Dad," and "Grandma." I had never done the whole "meet the parents" thing before and had zero interest in changing that for someone I literally just met.

While I'm usually great at small talk, the non-conversations that ensued only made the situation increasingly uncomfortable. Her father asked about my family, and I told him that I didn't really have a close relationship with them. Her mother asked about my career goals, and I explained that I had been unemployed and temping for the past year since graduating. These were topics I had covered time and again while casually dating over the past year, though not exactly the type of information I wanted to divulge to a complete stranger if it didn't mean I'd be getting laid.

When I was introduced to her uncle, rather than ask about my background or career endeavors, he simply stated, "Adrienne's like a daughter to me. Treat her right if you want this to last."

Thanks. While I'm sure she was great, I was suddenly less sure I wanted this to last, considering she just blindsided me with meeting her entire family and all.

Things just got more uncomfortable from there. Prior to eating, her family gathered for a pre-dinner prayer. Her father took the reins and began to thank God for the food and for bringing the family together. It was, to that point, pretty customary.

Then, he continued, "And God, I especially want to thank you for the newest addition to our family."

When everyone's eyes were closed, I looked at Adrienne and mouthed, "Are you pregnant?"

She mouthed back, "No, silly."

Her father continued, "We are all very grateful that you brought Chris into our lives."

Name-dropped in a family prayer less than two months after meeting the girl? That's got to be some kind of record. With that, I decided to speak only when spoken to, offering zero insight into whatever social skills I possessed, hoping to make these people find nothing worth revisiting in me.

"So what do you do, Chris?"

"Unemployed."

"What do you want to do?"

"Not sure."

"Do you want to teach?"

"No. Can't stand kids. No patience for them."

Apparently, Adrienne must have talked up my sarcasm, because they took every blunt and blatant response as me being charmingly witty.

"So, tell us how you met."

Jackpot. Adrienne had long mentioned that this was a story she would have preferred not sharing.

"Funny story," she started. "We met—"

"—At a bar," I cut her off before she could make something up.

"Oh my! They even finish each other's sentences," her mother acknowledged.

"Yes. We met at a bar," Adrienne restated, fearing that I'd go into further detail.

"I was actually on a date with her roommate," I continued. "She asked that I bring a friend for her friend, with her friend being your daughter."

Whether irritated or embarrassed, Adrienne got up and walked inside. With her daughter storming into the house, her mother piped up.

"It must have been fate. You two were meant to meet, and her friend was the catalyst that made it happen."

I felt like I stepped into *The Twilight Zone*.

I walked into the house and over to Adrienne, who was standing by a window.

"Hey, I'm sorry about that. I know you didn't want them to know."

She turned to me and smiled. "You know, I'm glad you told them. If that's how we were meant to meet, then so be it. You can't deny fate."

"At least we know you weren't adopted," I said.

"What?"

"Nothing. It's just that your mom said something along those same lines."

"She's never really approved of the guys I date, but I think she sees something in you. I do, too."

There was a pause, and I was hopeful that was as far as she was going to go with it. But she continued.

"She told me that you were the guy I was going to marry."

I stepped back. "You asked if I wanted to be exclusive, and I said yes, because exclusivity means that you and I agree to not sleep with or date anybody else while we continue getting to know one another."

I grabbed her left hand to try and make a point, but she assumed I'm trying to hold hands with her and interlocked fingers with me.

"Did we get drunk last night?" I asked.

She laughed and nodded her head.

"Let me rephrase," I lifted her hand so that it was eye level, "Were we so drunk that I put an invisible engagement ring on your finger and forgot about it?"

I started feeling around her left hand as she stared at me with a confused expression. Then, as if the crazy came back to her, her jaw dropped. What she said next nearly made mine drop, too.

"Oh my God! Do you have a ring?!"

I let go of her hand, shook my head in disbelief, and back-stepped away from her.

"Where are you going, baby?"

"This isn't what I signed up for. I'm out."

"But aren't you going to stay for the fireworks?"

Thanks, but I think I've seen enough of those for one day, as it is.

Six Emotions in Sixty Minutes

Lizzy Miles

Social scientists have identified six basic human emotions that we all express: sadness, disgust, anger, fear, surprise, and joy. On Valentine's Day, 2002, I experienced all these emotions within 60 minutes.

I was in grad school at the time and after a long day of classes, I felt sad. On my way home from class I tried to call my boyfriend Kevan to whine about my day. He didn't answer the home phone. This was back in the day before everyone had a cell phone. I had one and loved it, but I had friends like my husband who were holdouts.

"Why the heck would I want to be available at every second to anyone who wants to call? They can just leave a message on the answering machine."

I was disgusted that he did not answer the phone and invented a complete scenario for his whereabouts. I convinced myself he was at Plaza Fiesta Mexican happy hour shaking maracas with co-workers. He's had four cervezas by now. He forgot that it was Valentine's Day. What a jerk. Of course this was all invented by my hormonal female mind.

By the time I got home, I had worked myself into an angry frenzy. I could not believe he would go out on Valentine's Day. Did I mention that it was Valentine's Day? Yeah, perhaps I was a little obsessed with the holiday since we had been living together for over three years. Nevertheless, I had a crappy day, and he just made it worse by not being home.

When I pulled into the driveway, I noticed the garbage can was still outside. My heart sunk when I opened the garage door and his Jeep wasn't there. Part of me had hoped the happy hour scenario was just a delusion, but where else would he be?

I parked my car and walked out to the mailbox to get the mail. Junk. I walked in through the garage and flipped on the light switch. Nothing happened. I tried another switch and, again, nothing. It was pitch black in my house.

As my eyes adjusted, I could see small details. Over to my left I saw the butcher block from the kitchen was blocking the front door. The cats' chairs, which were normally in front of the kitchen windows, were pulled back. The front shutters were closed. There was no good reason for our front door to be barricaded. I was the *last* one to leave the house, and so many things were different from how it was when I left in the morning.

I did not know what to do. I couldn't hear anything in the house. I then recognized my cat was missing. Normally when I got home Daisy would be purring and weaving in and out between my legs. She wasn't there. Kevan wasn't there.

Panic set in. Suddenly, I felt I needed to get OUT OF THE HOUSE immediately. I quickly stepped back through the laundry room into the garage. The garage light didn't come on either. I opened the garage door and ran through the garage and into the street. My mind was racing. I wondered who I should call. The tears started to flow. I cursed my boyfriend for being a cell phone hold out. Then it occurred to me that our friend Teri was a happy hour regular and *always* carried her cell phone.

I decided to call Teri to see if she knew anything. She picked up on the second ring. I skipped the niceties and went straight towards interrogation. I asked if she was at happy hour. I asked if Kevan was there. The entire time I interrogated her, I was watching the house and sobbing hysterically.

Teri was concerned and a bit confused. She was at home watching television. She was not at happy hour and had no idea why I was calling, why I was crying, or why I was asking about Kevan. She did her best to sort things out and asked me what was going on. I told her in one breath, "Kevan's not home. I don't know where he is. I think someone is in my house."

This is the point at which I should probably admit to you that I did and still do watch a lot of true crime television shows. Teri would make for a good detective because she told me to calm down and she asked me to repeat slowly what I was telling her. I gave her the evidence that Kevan hadn't been home—the garbage can, the mail, the lights not working, and the furniture being moved.

Then I screamed.

The door to the house opened, and I saw a shadow of a man standing in my house. Then I heard his voice. It was Kevan. He said, "Elizabeth, come inside, it's alright."

Quickly, I told Teri to never mind because everything was okay and hung up. I was very confused, but I complied with Kevan and walked towards the house.

I reached Kevan and he led me inside. The lights were blazing and it took me a second to adjust. I looked around and everything seemed to be in order. I looked up at the fireplace mantle and there were red heart-shaped helium balloons and two bouquets of flowers. The house phone was ringing. Balloons? Flowers? There were construction paper letters on the wall above the fireplace. They said E I L Y V M. W Y M M? K. We used to talk in code when we worked together. I looked at Kevan and he was standing there next to me holding a beautiful platinum diamond ring in a little black box. Suddenly it all made sense.

We were not being robbed. He was asking me to marry him. Tears streamed down my face. Snot dripped from my nose. This was a set up and had all been planned. Kevan had been telling me all week about the "electrical problems." I was supposed to go in the dark house and go down to the basement and then turn on the power and be surprised. All the men he told about the plan thought it was a great idea. He did not get any women's opinions. Well, I was surprised for sure. Between the sobs, I told him yes and then he hugged me. He wiped my tears of fear and joy, and told me I had better answer the phone.

"ELIZABETH WHAT IS GOING ON?" Teri screamed into the phone.

I was suddenly calm. "It's ok, Kevan just asked me to marry him."

"Ooh my GOD! Congratulations! You better go. We'll talk tomorrow." She hung up.

That night I did not call anyone to tell them I was engaged. I was too exhausted. However, the next day by the time I got to work, the story of our home invasion turned engagement with my snot face ala *The Blair Witch Project* had made the rounds at the office.

We were married in September of that year. When you start out that way, there's nowhere to go but up!

Lizzy Miles changes her mind frequently about her name and her career identity, but she has always held true to her enthusiasm for written and oral storytelling. She has been published in a wide variety of formats including: award-winning Hallmark cards, academic journal articles, and retail training manuals. Circle her on Google+, and she'll flood your stream with posts about death and dying, Muppets, and the U.S. Postal Service.

Dyngus Day: Flogging for Love
Jenn Dlugos

When I tell people about Dyngus Day, they usually
think I am making it up. I am not. Dyngus Day
falls on the day after Easter and can best be
described as a Polish matchmaking holiday.
Traditionally, single Polish men run through the
town, dousing maidens with buckets of water and
smacking them on the legs with pussy willow
branches. The women respond much like anyone
would to an assault—by throwing pots and pans at
the men. The next day, the roles are reversed, and
the women assault the men in the same manner.
In theory, if you assault the same person who
assaulted you, you have found your soul mate.

This explains the existence of Polish jokes.

I grew up in Buffalo, NY, a town that holds the
distinction of having the largest Dyngus Day
celebration on this side of the world. Buffalo has
the second largest Polish population in the country
(the first being Chicago), so Dyngus Day in Buffalo
is on par with St. Patrick's Day in Boston. Since I
am 100% Polish and single, it's mandatory for me
to participate in the revelries, bruises from pussy
willow assaults notwithstanding.

My most memorable Dyngus Day occurred in
college. That year, I participated in the festivities
with some college friends. My friend Bea was down
with it immediately. Bea is so Polish that her real
name is Bogna, but she went with Bea because she
thought Bogna sounded like the name of a hobbit
lunch lady from *Lord of the Rings*. Dyngus Day was
Bea's personal Holy Day of Obligation. I had just

met Bea that semester, but I knew two things about her: the last time she was single was in third grade and she never dated a man for more than a month. I once requested that she make a wall calendar out of her past lovers, so we could take a stroll down memory lane with Mr. January or Mr. April. My friends Amanda and Chuck also joined the Dyngus party bus. They hailed from New York City and were our designated Dyngus virgins.

Chuck's friend Melanie was scheduled to be in attendance, however on the way to Chuck's dorm, she got into a fender bender with an ice cream truck. Ice cream trucks are not an indigenous species to Buffalo. They migrate from the South in the summer and disappear in the winter. Kind of like killer bees, actually. Melanie managed to locate the sole winter survivor that was on its way to a church function and plowed it off the road with her 1994 Ford Escort. The U.S. government should get Melanie on the killer bee problem.

In retrospect, the universe could not possibly have given us a more sinister omen for our night than the murder of an ice cream truck in Buffalo in April. But being college students, we couldn't be bothered with things like signs, seals, or omens. Our primary concern was to procure alcohol, and Polish vodka was first on the agenda.

The Dyngus Day celebrations occur in Polonia, the historical Polish district of Buffalo. The residential area is no longer Polish, but it still has the old Polish churches, restaurants, and the famed Broadway Market, which is the one-stop shop for all of your kielbasa and pierogi needs. All the bars and restaurants participate in the revelries, but the largest celebration is at the old Buffalo Central terminal, a former train terminal now famous for being named by *Ghost Hunters* as one of the nation's most haunted locations. Visiting the terminal on Dyngus Day marked the first time I ever heard "We're not Going to Take It" by Twisted Sister played on an accordion. A magical time of year, indeed.

The four of us secured our Pussywillow Pass for the festivities and waited for the vodka-sponsored trolley to take us to our first alcohol-laden destination. The scene was pretty typical. As Amanda applied a heavy layer of eye shadow, she grilled me on the ingredients of Polish cuisine, recounting her extensive food allergies in gory detail. Chuck wondered if his new shoes would withstand the water-gun assaults. And Bea flirted with a fellow vodka-trolley passenger who wore a tee-shirt that read "Pat My Pierogi." The problems didn't really start until we walked into the first party stop and Amanda got smacked in the face with a bouquet of pussy willows.

The bouquet-wielding gentleman apologized profusely in both Polish and English. It wasn't even a legitimate Dyngus love-connection attempt. He was just delivering this batch of love whips to the bar. No harm, no foul, we assured him. Bea reassured him by giving him her phone number.

"My eye feels funny." Amanda said as she plucked a pussy willow bud out of her hair. We responded like any typical concerned college kids—we bought her a shot of vodka.

Within an hour, the revelries kicked up to full speed. A Polish band whipped up some feisty polkas. Squirt guns and pussy willows were in full assault mode. Highly suggestive signs on the walls read "Do Not Flog or Squirt the Workers." After Amanda bolted to the bathroom for the 10th time to check on her eyeball, Bea deserted us to collect more contributions for her personal Single Men of Western New York phonebook. After a few moments, Chuck nudged me and gestured to a young guy at the end of the bar.

"What do you think?"

I turned my head. "For me or for you?"

"Me."

Honestly, I was relieved he even asked. Chuck and I used to date. Our relationship ended unceremoniously two months earlier when he came out of the closet. Our friends were not surprised. None of them actually thought he was gay; it's just that we were already the most incompatible couple on the planet. He wanted to get married right out of college. I wanted to get married when I grow too old to feed myself. He was 5'2; I am 6'0 tall. He wanted seven kids. I wanted a dog. He was allergic to dogs. After he came out, two of my friends asked if we were still dating. At that point, it just seemed like one more obstacle we'd have to work through. This was the first time since we became "just friends" that he asked for my opinion on a possible suitor.

Chuck furrowed his brow, "I'm getting the gay vibe, but I'm not completely sure. What do you think?" Given our history, this was probably the stupidest question he could have asked me.

"Chuck, if you recall, my gaydar is not be the most

accurate instrument."

I recounted the rules of the holiday to him. Being rejected on Dyngus Day simply means you don't get assaulted. Win or lose, you win. That was enough to convince him. He gulped his liquid courage and walked over to the intriguing young man. I wished him well on his quest and ordered myself a Polish feast. Ten minutes later I was doubled over the bar, choking on a pierogi.

So, this is how I'm going to die, I thought. *Choking on the food of my people.*

The coughing fit lasted for five minutes. The bartender asked if I was OK, and I nodded yes, even though I was clearly not. My Polish family instilled in me a pathological fear of making a scene in public. Receiving the Heimlich maneuver from a complete stranger is equal to being locked in stocks for public ridicule in the town square. The bartender looked skeptical, but I reassured him once again that I was OK. I figured by the time the coroner showed up, I'd be too dead to care that I was making a scene.

By the hand of Saint Dyngus I miraculously recovered. Still blinded by my choke-induced tears, Chuck bolted up to me, his face reddened with embarrassment.

"We have to go, *right now*," he urged.

Chuck's mystery man was actually a newly ordained priest who had just taken his priestly vows five days earlier. He came to the Polish revelries to celebrate his new life of sacred celibacy with his proud parents. When Chuck approached him with some sort of suggestive comment, he came face-to-face with the sacred young man's white priest's collar.

After hitting on a priest and encountering a deadly pierogi, we decided to head to the party at the terminal. Chuck pulled Bea away from the band's lead accordion player. Amanda, however, was nowhere to be found. I finally tracked her down in the bathroom, where she was crying hysterically in front off the bathroom mirror. Both of her eyes were beet-red and she was breaking out in a heavy rash on her eyelids. Bea rushed her to the emergency room for what we assumed to be a reaction to the unintentional pussy willow assault. As it turned out, Amanda does not have an allergy to pussy willows, but she does have a severe allergy to the sparkly eye shadow she bought from the dollar store. At least the night ended on a romantic note. The next weekend, Bea and Amanda went on a double date with the E.R. nurse and his roommate.

Chuck and I continued to the terminal. Neither one of us attempted another Dyngus love match, but we had a hell of a time. We ran into several kids from our classes and partied until there was no more party to be had. The only other awkward moment of the night occurred when I was chatting up a fellow classmate, and his very, *very* drunk girlfriend loudly accused him of hitting on me. His girlfriend had a long history of being a jealous drunk, so he simply held her hand,

"Calm down," he whispered. "That's her boyfriend over there." He pointed to Chuck. Dammit. I knew I forgot to send someone our break-up memo.

"That guy?" she said, following her boyfriend's pointing finger. "Jesus Christ, I'm drunk, and even I can tell he's gay."

That Dyngus Day had many lessons. I will never buy eye makeup from a dollar store. I will not hit on a man who is wearing a black shirt unless I am sure he is not a priest. Most importantly, I learned that my gaydar may not be broken after all. I just need a stronger prescription for beer goggles.

SECTION FIVE

My Special Day of Woe

Happy Birthday to Me
Jim Frazier

Is April Fools' Day considered a holiday?

Well to those of us who were lucky enough to be born on that day and suffer the years of woeful humiliation that goes along with it, it sure as hell should be a holiday.

I'm sure I could think of many stories about the teasing, torture, and ridicule that I suffered at the hands of friends, family, and complete strangers through the years. There's nothing like being an overweight kid in junior high with bad acne whose mother who sends you to school wearing your sister's hand-me-down red bell bottom jeans, and the teacher announces in front of a classroom filled with jocks and cheerleaders that it's your birthday.

Fast forward to 1997. My life hadn't improved very much. I was eight months out of my marriage, dirt poor, and living in my brother's basement. A cross between 1970's shit-brown, shag-carpet chic and post-war Bosnia. Needless to say, I spent a lot of time at the office.

As it happened, I was at my office on the eve of my birthday that year. That was also the night we were hit with a late season snow storm that blanketed the Boston area with 36 inches of snow.

I left the office just before midnight. There was about a foot of snow on the ground and zero visibility. I figured out pretty quickly that there was no way I was going to make it to my nice cold dungeon at my brother's house, so I decided to detour to my sister's. I got to the end of her street only to find that it hadn't been plowed yet. So I did what all New Englanders do in that situation, I backed up 30 feet and floored it into the unplowed snow.

I skidded and fishtailed up the street until I reached my sister's house. There was no place to park, so I aimed for her front door and drove as fast as I could into the pile of snow on her front lawn. Yes, the back half the truck was still in the street, but I didn't really care.

I crashed on my sister's couch for a solid three hours, until she woke me up at 4:30 a.m. She needed me to move my truck so she could go to work. I asked her if she was kidding, but she wasn't.

I got up, put on my wet socks and shoes and walked back out into the blizzard. Fortunately, no plows had come yet so my truck was still intact. Unfortunately, no plows had come yet so there was now a good 20 inches of snow on the street.

It took me about an hour, but I got my truck out of her front yard and proceeded to drive around the block to give her time to back her car out. Driving around the block, I managed to get stuck two or three times. Each time I was able to rock my truck back and forth, drive and reverse, drive and reverse, until regaining forward momentum.

Then, I hit a patch of ice hidden deep under the snow, and I was stuck. My wheels were spinning and all the rocking back and forth wasn't going to get me out of there. But I'm from New England, plus I'm Irish, which means I often mistake stubbornness for determination.

So I rocked that truck. I rocked the shit out of it. Back and forth, drive and reverse. What's that, the smell of burning rubber? I'm sure it's just the tires digging in. Banging sounds coming from the engine? It just means the truck is working hard. Smoke pouring out from under the hood? I'm sure it's nothing. Every single warning light on the dash board was lit up. It was very Christmassy.

Then a familiar voice called out to me, "I don't think that it's supposed to smoke like that."

I shut off the truck and discovered an old childhood friend standing nearby. His name was Mark and he, too, lived in the neighborhood.

I responded, "Are you sure?" and we both started laughing.

Mark had actually made the two-hour trek into Boston that morning only to be told to go home. Everything was closed.

He jumped into the truck and we discussed the predicament. Neither one of us knew anything about fixing trucks, but we figured we'd give it a try anyway. I popped the hood and we did what guys do, we stared at the engine and scratched our heads.

As we waited for the engine to cool off, we hid from the snow under the open hood and used the overheated engine to keep warm. Mark started singing "Let It Snow" to keep our spirits up. I joined in, and we sang at the top of our lungs. When the smoke cleared, I noticed a rubber belt hanging off the engine. I told Mark that I didn't think it was supposed to be hanging like that. He shrugged his shoulders and suggested we try to put it back on.

As we tried to figure out how to put the belt back on, we continued to sing. Then out of nowhere came another voice. "Would you boys like something hot to drink?" The woman who lived in the house that I was stuck in front of had brought us out two cups of coffee.

We thanked her and apologized for being a nuisance.

She pointed to the bay window on the front of her house and commented, "Are you kidding, my kids have been watching you for an hour and singing along."

We looked up and saw three little kids in their pajamas waving to us. She said the kids wanted to hear us sing "Santa Claus is Coming to Town," and so we happily obliged.

After a few verses of "Santa Claus" and then "Jingle Bells," we somehow got the belt back on the engine, and the truck miraculously started up again. Mark helped me push it forward and we were back in business. We returned the empty cups to our grateful audience and waved goodbye as we drove off.

I gave Mark a ride home and thanked him for his help. He wished me a happy birthday and headed up his driveway.

As I drove home I thought about this cruel April

Fools' joke that Mother Nature had played on me. I tried to look on the bright side. The worst of my day was behind me.

I was wrong.

Unfortunately, there is a limit on the length of this essay, so I can't write about how my mother guilted me into driving 25 miles out of my way, so I could spend the afternoon shoveling my parents' driveway even though they weren't actually going anywhere. Or getting home that night to find that my brother hadn't touched the 50-foot ski slope he called a driveway.

Suffice it to say, Mother Nature had the last laugh as I spent the last few minutes of my birthday shoveling my brother's driveway in the freezing cold, wearing the same soaking wet clothes I'd had on for almost 36 hours and quietly singing "Happy Birthday to Me."

Jim Frazier is a divorced father of two not-quite-yet adult children. He is employed at a Financial Institution as an office manager. After years of being told by family, friends, and his therapist that he "really needs" to write down his stories, he has finally decided to listen to them.

How to Throw an Unsuccessful Birthday Party for Your Girlfriend

Dale Rappaneau

Step 1: Invite all of your friends, what few you know. Hype up the party with buzz words like "sick" and "bumping" and "lots of hot drunk girls." Create a Facebook event, and then forget to change it from a public to private event, allowing everyone and their grandmother the opportunity to come party at your place.

Step 2: Hire a DJ. But before you wade into the Craigslist cesspool, ask your friends if they know anyone with a "beast sound system." Make sure to use those exact words, so they think you're down with the lyrical lingo. Honestly, though, you're just going for noise quantity, not sound quality. Any Average Joe with a pair of speakers better than your $20 Walmart junkers could do the job.

Step 3: Buy the booze. Think long and hard about the alcohol you purchase for the party, because Hypnotiq may look tempting on the shelf, all blue and expensive, but when Rolph, the asshole who asks if he can date your girlfriend after "you've had your turn," sucks a whole bottle clean, only to spew a blueberry fountain on your white carpets followed by a second bout in your bed, where he passes out, leaving you to clean up the mess while listening to his half-conscious apologies, you'll wish the Hypnotiq had been passed over for something less colorful. Like well vodka. Let Rolph suck on that.

Step 4: Demand each guest pay $5 to enter the party. Ask one of your larger, more intimidating friends to collect the money at the door. Just make sure it's not someone prone to taking ecstasy, because you may soon discover the bouncer literally bouncing on the dance floor while tossing all your door money on a gaggle of women, one of which is yelling, "Men, come to me." You better believe Rolph is one of those men.

Step 5: Leave the front door unlocked during the party. Better yet—get too drunk to remember whether or not you locked the door. The cacophonous music flowing out of your home will be an attractant for anyone looking to crash a party, such as three 40-something German dudes with a habit for showing off their abs to any ladies shallow enough to indulge. You may later find one of those German dudes standing over one of your passed out female friends, just standing there, staring at her defenseless body. He'll have eyes similar to an addict staring at an unclaimed bag of cocaine, all glazed over and wild and wondering if he could, in fact, get away with whatever it is that those eyes are thinking about. When you tell him to leave, he'll show you his abs. When you shake your head, saying no, I don't want to see your abs, he'll yell angry German words and rush back to his two other foreign friends. Yeah, definitely leave the door unlocked. You'd hate to miss this part.

Step 6: Mingle with strangers. Not much to explain about this step.

Step 7: Monitor the party. Between shots and beer bongs, walk around the party and watch for anyone making trouble. Like those German dudes, one of which, a different one than last time, you'll find following your girlfriend out of a dark room while she's buttoning up her shirt. Your stupid drunken head will tell you that she's been servicing this German man's wienerschnitzel, but really that's your frustration from Rolph's earlier comment coming to a head. You'll even have the audacity to ask her if she's been fooling around with the German. She won't respond—not verbally, but her gaping mouth, squinted eyes, and furrowed brow will be a shining example of angered disbelief. She'll then go walk to Rolph and start up a conversation, just to spite you.

Step 8: Play a prank on your girlfriend. After the previous insult, she will have descended into a booze-ridden downward spiral ending with her passed out in your bedroom. That's when you'll get the brilliant idea to fill one of her hands with shaving cream while tickling her nose with a feather. At first, it'll work: she'll twitch, groan, and even open one of her eyes. But then she'll begin to convulse, because her drunk mind coming back to reality so quickly will be too much for her stomach to handle, and she'll begin to throw up all over your bed (the same one that Rolph will later throw up on). Sure, you'll pick her up, shamble over to the toilet, and get her head over the bowl, but not before her stomach purges its contents all down your shirt and pants.

Step 9: Drink. Honestly, after all that has happened during this unsuccessful birthday party, you'll need a drink. Maybe two or even six. In fact, go ahead and drink so much that you end up shirtless, wearing a Dalmatian-print bathrobe and plaid pants that have the face of Grumpy, one of the seven dwarves from Snow White, plastered on the ass. It's around this time that you'll black out, waking up sometime later on the bathroom floor, two friends trying to get you back into bed. Instead of accepting their help, you'll apologize, over and over, to their sneakers, not looking them in the face, not capable of lifting your head and staring at another human being in the eyes. Why? Well, because you've successfully thrown an utterly unsuccessful birthday party for your girlfriend—a true disaster that will be remembered in half memories for years to come. Congratulations.

Dale Rappaneau is currently planning to hike all of the Appalachian Trail, in 2013, which should supply him with loads of woeful stories. Stay tuned for details.

What a F'in Ripoff!
Colleen McCauley Coughlan

As adults, many people view their birthday as a sign of impending death. They pretend they are 29 when they are 45. They seethe with jealousy at people who actually are 29 and have their whole lives ahead of them. Well, that is not me! My birthday is not only a day of celebration, but I turn it into a month-long extravaganza. Daily updates. Reminders to buy me something. Promises to get fucked up and sing karaoke. When I plan my birthday, I spare no expense. Of course, my husband has to pay for everything, but I refuse to see that it's "our" money when it comes to my presents.

Another awesome thing about my birthday is that it is two days before Halloween. I don't actually have to share the day, but it's close enough to make my birthday famous by association. I had about a billion costume parties growing up. Now that I am a mom, I can see how happy it must have made my friends' moms to get more than one use out of their kids' costumes.

My last birthday approached with my usual enthusiasm and annoying behavior. 4 weeks! 3 weeks! 2 weeks! 1 more week, people! WOOOO! Out went the "Come to my house and get all fucked up and sing karaoke," email. YES! YES! YES! My friends couldn't wait. My birthday was gonna kick Halloween's ass.

Until Mother Nature intervened. I am not quite sure why she had to barge into my life, or even the month of October, for that matter. But the weather reports started pouring in. A blizzard was coming to Massachusetts, in October, on my birthday. What the shit is that all about?

Maybe they will be wrong, I mean, weather people are like, ALWAYS wrong, right?

The cancellation emails and calls came in left and right. My heart fractured, my birthday balloon deflated right in my sad, yet sweet, face. I wanted to punch snow in the face.

"I'll still come over!" my friend Robyn promised.

YAY! I'll get a lot of turns for karaoke with only one friend to play with.

"It's just snow! We'll be there!" my friend, Nita, promised. I felt a little better. I'll have three friends at my party. And a blizzard. Sigh.

We commenced with the festivities, food, music, and beer in abundance. I love my friends who aren't complete babies when it comes to a Nor'easter in October.

My husband had to plow, so he could only stop by for a little while to celebrate with us, which really meant he ate a bunch a food before leaving.

"Can I see you in the other room?" he asked.

"Um, OK, but I am trying to have fun here." I replied with my usual charm.

"Well, you see, the thing is, I, um, well, I flunked your birthday."

The happiness balloon was deflating rapidly. He got the blank stare. And a very long and uncomfortable silence followed.

"What do you mean you flunked my birthday?"

You know when a woman gets upset, her voice switches to a weird shrill that dogs fear and makes children scatter? Yeah, so does the husband.

"Well, you know, with the storm coming, I just kind of forgot."

"Well, my birthday has been coming all year! You went out today to get your plow! You were out!"

"I know! I'm sorry! But I'll make it up to you! We will go away for St Patrick's day!"

"Tim, we were already going away for St Patrick's day."

"Well…."

"You need to go plow now."

Off he went, probably kind of scared for his life, as he should have been.

I managed to soldier on, partying with my friends, stuffing my feelings of disappointment and despair into the far corners of my mind. And we had fun. We sang and ate and drank and had a pretty good time, even if there was some kind of conspiracy against me having a happy birthday. We went to bed at about 2:00 a.m. (For the record, yes I do indeed still rock.) I drifted off to sleep the slumber of a drunk chick.

I woke up far too early, mostly due to the urgency of 15 beers tearing me out of my slumber to hit the loo. As I returned to bed, I looked out the window to see what that douche Mother Nature had left behind.

I saw our cars covered in snow. But Robyn's car got an extra special surprise. A big, ginormous tree limb right through the roof of her car. Do I dare mention it's her brand new car? Do I mention that this chick is totally into cars, and her vehicle is probably ranked higher on her love scale than her husband? Do I just run away and start a new life down the Florida Keys? It was very tempting at that point.

I broke the news. We shed some tears, then laughed the maniacal laugh of insane people. It took a week to get our power back and 6 months to get Robyn's car back. Plus, I am still waiting for my birthday cake.

Colleen "Don't forget my maiden name is McCauley" Coughlan is currently a stay at home mom and day drinker. She decided to try stand-up comedy for her mid-life crisis because it's cheaper than breast augmentation, and she likes to avoid small talk with her family at night. Colleen's acting career peaked in 1997 when she had the small role of "Cathy" in Good Will Hunting. Colleen was excited to submit this essay because it gave her a reason to lock herself alone in her room and "write" which is also known as "watch endless TV shows On Demand." Colleen is actively searching for a corporate sponsor to avoid going "legit" AKA "working."

Birthday Bloody Birthday
Danny Gallagher

Kids look forward to birthdays for a lot of selfish reasons but deep down, they all have the same hope. They actually look forward to getting older.

The rest of us dread the passing of another year of not dying, but the young ones look forward to their birthdays with wide eyes full of stars and wonder. They get to do all the things that parents and grown-ups do like drive a car, stay up late, and drink strange brown liquids that make them talk funny and cry over football games.

Even when they first learn the sad fact that everything born into this world will eventually die, they somehow put that bad news aside to jump for joy at every minute that ticks closer to their next birthday. Either the joy of getting older has clouded their brains or our education system needs more overhauling than we think it does.

My unbridled joy for birthdays lasted exactly six years. As a matter of fact, it lasted right up until the day of my 6th birthday. It was a small affair with junk food that could give a horse diabetes and two parents who loved their oldest child enough to celebrate the day they received the greatest gift God could give them. The second greatest gift is an epidural.

My folks announced that they were going to order pizza for dinner, let me shove as much cake as I could into my tiny body, and then end the evening with a viewing of my all-time favorite movie *Ghost Busters*. The coolest part is that all of this was taking place on a school night. So not only was I growing a year older, but I was also going to be able to tell all of my jealous schoolmates that I was allowed to do the three things their parents would never let them do on a school night until they hit puberty and learn how to clear the browser history on their laptop.

The saddest part is that that moment never happened. In fact, I should have considered myself lucky that I was able to speak to them at all.

All I had to do to kick off this evening was to wash my hands. I had been playing outside and being a precocious five about to be six-year-old, I somehow managed to find and sample every pile of dirt in the parish. I wasted no time with pizza on the way and took to my mother's orders the way an army private takes to his drill sergeant's orders to clean the head, although the private would probably skip less unless his goal was to get out of the army.

I lived in a typical suburban home with a couple of bedrooms and one and a half bathrooms. My bathroom, for some reason, had the tallest bathroom sink in the state. My parents had given me a step stool so I could reach the sink without any problems, but I was getting older and having to use the stepstool seemed like a 32-year-old having to wear a bib in public that wasn't part of some bizarre man-baby fetish.

I was practically a man in the eyes of a kid. In a couple of years, my folks would teach me how to tie my own shoes or drive or develop the psychosocial skills needed to convince a girl to let a shooting star fall from the sky and land in her stomach to produce a baby for me. The latter belief would ruin another birthday down the line.

So rather than take the easy way, I used the handles of the linen drawers as a miniature ladder to climb up to the sink. The bathroom counter had the sink on one end adjacent to the toilet and a large porcelain area that was clearly meant for small children with easily broken bones to sit on so they could wash their hands, brush their teeth, or play in the sink. I finished scrubbing up for my scrumptious banquet. I began to climb down not realizing that my hands were still wet. My right hand lost its grip on the porcelain causing me to turn and fall towards the toilet. I could feel my chin hit the toilet seat and break my fall but any pain it caused was erased from my mind after the back of my mop topped head slammed down on the tile floor. The very next memory I had was my panicked father staring over me and screaming, "He's bleeding! He's bleeding!"

I tried to ask what was the matter, but when I said it, it sounded like someone was holding my tongue with their thumb and forefinger as I said it. My quick thinking old man scooped me off the floor and carried me to the sofa while my mother threw some ice into a clean dish towel and placed it over my mouth. I remember one of them saying, "I'll call for an ambulance. You go look for the rest of his tongue."

The ambulance took forever to get to the house. The pizza showed up long before the ambulance did. In fact, they refused to take me to the hospital since they didn't know how to treat me. The only way the paramedics could have been slightly helpful was if they brought the complimentary side of "Crazy Bread" the delivery guy forgot.

We had to drive ourselves to the emergency room where I finally learned that my tongue was still intact but had a giant split in the middle of it in the shape of the top two thirds of a triangle. The doctor wasn't much help either. He somehow stopped the bleeding, or it stopped on its own. But, my tongue couldn't be sewn back together. The only advice he gave to my parents was that I shouldn't eat solid foods and to only feed me soup and mashed potatoes. I may have been six-years-old at the time, but I distinctly remember wanting to jump off the gurney and punch the bastard square in the crotch.

By the time we got home, the pizza was cold and inedible. The cake couldn't be eaten no matter how hard I tried to convince my Mom I could make it a liquid by dipping every bite in milk. The movie went unwatched since I had to go straight to bed and rest. I couldn't even sleep in my new race car pajamas that were now caked in my own blood.

Eventually my tongue healed and left an interesting scar I still have to this day. We were able to celebrate my sixth birthday after we got the all clear from a qualified doctor. Birthdays were still fun from then on, but they didn't seem like momentous milestones after my scary sixth. Getting older felt like you were becoming more fragile or defective somehow.

The only hope we have when our time comes is that maybe we'll get cake.

Danny Gallagher is a writer, reporter, humorist and all around nice guy living in Texas. He has contributed pieces to several magazines and newspapers including Maxim, The Christian Science Monitor and The Chicago Tribune's "Red Eye" as well as several humor pieces for websites such as Maxim.com, Cracked.com, Topless Robots.com, Mental Floss and CBS' Mancave Daily. He also writes comedy sketches for the Shadowbox Comedy and Rock 'n Roll Theater in Columbus, Ohio and is an associate editor and regular contributor for GameTrailers' Side Mission blog. He can be found on the web at **www.danny gallagher.net**, *on Twitter @thisisdannyg and in bars enjoying strange brown liquids that make him yell at whatever happens to be on the television.*

SECTION SIX

Home for the Woe-i-days

Turkey Bird Flu
Mike Ryan

When society is inspired by collectively high
emotion, things sometimes happen that seem
completely reasonable in the moment, but utterly
mystifying and illogical in hindsight.
In that hindsight, my bird flu Thanksgiving seemed
pretty ridiculous. But at the time…

It was 2009, and Thanksgiving was going to be a
little different for me that year. I come from a
small family, where T-Day was a very standard,
predictable set of rituals that my sister, aunt, and I
took part in, under the direction of my mother.
But in 2009, I was spending Thanksgiving with my
girlfriend (at the time—but that's a different tale of
Woe). My sister and aunt each had different last-
minute emergencies, which left Mom by herself.
Recent dental surgery meant she wouldn't even
have a turkey for company. Maybe some turkey
soup.

So, we determined that Turkey Day would provide
the perfect opportunity for my mom to finally meet
my girlfriend and her sprawling family of cousins,
nephews, in-laws, step-exes and other happy-go-
lucky relatives-once-removed. Even fate seemed
complicit in the plan to bring my mom into the
fold—the site of Girlfriend-Family-Gathering '09
was one county over from the obscure New
Hampshire town my mom had retired to.

Now, I was a little nervous about making a good
impression on these folks, even though I'd met
some of them before, so I can only imagine how
my mom felt about it. But ultimately, it beat out

the turkey soup, and she agreed to come.

We booked a hotel, with a lovely pool and hot tub, right down the road from the site of the festivities. We drove up. We checked in. And somewhere along the way, I started to sneeze.

I've had the sniffles before. I was also running a low fever, so I knew I was getting a cold. What I'd forgotten, was that the Bird Flu was causing a lot of nervousness right at that time, casting suspicion on any sniffling stranger.

I had no kids, so I didn't realize that every parent in the U.S. had just received flyers and pamphlets, ferried home by an army of underage postal carriers, about the dangers and symptoms of Bird Flu. Half of Asia, and Michael Jackson, who was still with us, were wearing facemasks in public for protection.

My mom is both a cautious type and a doctor. So when she issues medical advice, everybody listens. They should. Except this time.

She heard I had the sniffles, and recommended immediately that I should not go near children. The family agreed. So did I, since giving Bird Flu to a flock of kids would be pretty much the worst thing I could imagine. Unfortunately, the result was that I was effectively banned from Turkey Day.
So, my mom met my girlfriend and her family without me. They had, by all accounts a wonderful Thanksgiving together, sprinkled with questions from the youngest clan members along the lines of, "Who's that lady?"

I sat in the hotel room and waited for the sniffles

to go away. A *Star Wars* rerun was on the TV. In the spirit of non-contagion, I didn't use the great pool or the hot tub or the gym. The hotel, set up as a ski resort, was completely deserted, every sound echoing down the empty hallways. And just before the Death Star got blown up, the cable went out.

The family wrapped up a bunch of leftovers for me —but, although Mom and my girlfriend both stopped in to check on my symptoms, each thought the other had the leftovers. I got a protein bar.

I didn't turn out to have Bird Flu. I was fine 48 hours later. But it still felt like the birds had gotten their Thanksgiving revenge.

Mike Ryan makes websites and has written ads for 20 years. His hobbies include traveling, filmmaking, scriptwriting, computer programming, and traveling. One time at band camp, he optioned a screenplay.

The Year I Got Socks for Christmas

Scott Sevener

The year was 1995.

It was a cold and blustery winter in Northern
Michigan, namely because there's no such thing as
a green Christmas when you live in Northern
Michigan. Instead, it starts snowing sometime just
before Halloween and if you're lucky, Mother
Nature finally decides to give it a rest by the
following Easter. This year she had been
particularly brutal, as noted by the mountainous
snow drifts that Mom had to plow through in the
minivan to drive me to school each morning.

Now I was merely a freshman in high school,
meaning that while I was technically starting to
grow up, I was still very much filled with all of the
angst and stubbornness and blatant cynicism that
ultimately made me a teenager. Case in point—
here we were in the middle of December with
temperatures in the single digits and snow drifts
higher than most cars, and yet nonetheless I
insisted on wearing sandals to school. Not exactly
my finest hour, intellectually speaking.

There were probably about half a dozen of us in
my class that did this—we were what you might
refer to today as "idiots," at least with regards to
footwear preference despite adverse weather
conditions. But you know teenagers, they'll do
anything to be different, even if that means getting
frostbite. And yet somehow throughout the course
of that year-and-a-half phase, miraculously

I didn't lose any extremities to the icy cold, thanks in no doubt to my secret weapon—wool socks.

As this particular Christmas rapidly approached, I found myself to some extent indifferent with regards to what people got me for presents that year. I was pretty busy at the time between starting to really notice girls and simultaneously being absolutely petrified to talk to them. Needless to say, my mind was thusly focused elsewhere. When family asked me what I'd like to find under the tree, my typical response was simply the classic teenage "I dunno…" or "Whatever…" Frankly, it's a wonder I managed to get anything at all that holiday season.

However, it seems that through all of said teenage apathy, one unique suggestion did somehow slip through the cracks. Despite being a blatant display of sarcastic intent, said suggestion was followed to the degree that anyone who has ever had to tolerate teenage smart-assery could dream. Low and behold, when it came time to open presents from my extended family, sure enough I opened a small and compactly-shaped package to find that one of my relatives had actually given me socks for Christmas.

Of course, there was little argument to be made—I mean, technically "they were what I had asked for," and they did proceed to keep my feet moderately toasty throughout the remainder of my inclination to wear inappropriate footwear. But more importantly, there was a lesson learned that afternoon as I sat there with my cousins, morosely holding my new socks as they excitedly tore open Nerf guns and remote-controlled helicopters and countless other awesome gifts that quite distinctly weren't socks. That lesson was this—don't be a smartass when someone asks you what you want for Christmas. They just might be a smartass, too.

And you'd better believe that the following year, yours truly was much more specific about his holiday desires, even if it meant just asking for gift cards and figuring it out later on my own time.

Returning to school from winter break was tough because, well, a gift like socks doesn't exactly put you at the top of the bragging list. But you know what they say—what Christmas gifts don't kill you only make you stronger.

Of course, there was also that year when one of my uncles "accidentally" swapped my present for a box full of bricks. But, we'll save that one for another day.

My Kingdom for a Potholder
Jessica Pinkman

I knew I should have stayed home.

I make the "I'm staying home" declaration to myself every holiday. And every year I try to get my sister Holly to go on strike with me.

"Say you're running out for cigarettes, but don't come back until January 2nd," I tell her.

She always refuses, muttering something about there isn't enough insurance on the house to withstand her absence. Holly has been married for over 30 years. She has a boatload of kids. I stopped counting after four. Since she was the only one procreating, our family holidays were moved to her house many years ago. It started as a convenient way not to drag the kids to each of the grandparents. Now, it's still a tradition. Unfortunately tradition also means dealing with her in-laws.

Holly's sister-in-law Mary hasn't quite grasped the "bring a dish" concept. Every holiday, Holly runs around franticly trying to make a six-course meal on four burners, and Mary will walk in with a block of cheese and an entire Hickory Farms sausage for my sister to plate up. For summer holidays she comes to the door with a full watermelon, like a caveman making a peace offering. The green bean casserole arrives in cans. She never even brings a baking dish to put it in. This dreaded casserole "tradition" delays dinner by 30-45 minutes every time.

Holly's brother-in-law Mark is on the other end of

the spectrum. A good 99% of the time, he doesn't bring anything. The one time he did, he set Holly's house on fire. Apparently he was annoyed that his dish was taking too long to cook and jacked up the temperature in Holly's oven without telling her. This threatened to turn our turkey into a 22-pound hockey puck, but the apricots cooking for the apricot pie were the true victims. In fact, we started a new tradition of *Apricots Roasting on an Open Fire*.

The in-laws are annoying, but we have learned that as long as there is no "disturbance in the Force," everyone stays mostly well fed and happy, except for my sister who needs to check into a celebrity rehab clinic for "exhaustion" after every fun family holiday. This Easter, the disturbance in the Force came in the form of Holly's foot surgery. The week before the holiday, she was off of complete bed rest, but she still had a cast and couldn't put pressure on her foot. The Easter dinner was threatened, and no one was more nervous than sister-in-law Mary.

"Do you think I'll need to have dinner at my house?" Mary asked. By the tone in her voice, you'd think we asked her if we could open a meth lab in her basement.

The Thursday before Easter it was decided Mary would have to host Easter this year. But, here is the kicker…even though it was at Mary's house, it was still expected that Holly cook the entire meal. I suppose in a world where caveman watermelon peace offerings are an appropriate way to "bring a dish," being asked to cook a meal, put it in a car, and cart it over to someone's house is considered to be a favor to you. Actually, Holly probably got off easy. Most cavemen would just lop off her foot and feed it to the wild boar they are fattening up to use as the holiday ham.

Holly is well-organized. You have to be with whatever number of children she has. She managed to get most of the meal prepared ahead of time with a little help from me and the kids. She told me to pack everything for the dinner including salt and pepper shakers, silverware, and paper napkins. I laughed at the overkill. Who doesn't have salt and pepper shakers? I really should have known better.

Holly called Mary to tell her the ham was coming over to her house to cook. This sent Mary in a tailspin. It became apparent that Mary's oven may as well be an alien spacecraft in her kitchen. Holly had to go over the instructions line by line starting with "the dial on the stove determines the temperature." We drew straws to see who would drive the ham over to Mary's house. I drew the short straw.

When I arrived, Mary pointed to the oven and said, "It's right there," before promptly running off to the other end of the house. I suddenly understood my sister's overkill with packing. Mary's kitchen was completely empty—no pots, utensils, or plates. Did I land in *Swiss Family Robinson*? Would we be eating out of tortoise shells?

I managed to find one serving platter that was covered with so much dust it may have actually come from King Tut's tomb. The instructions on the microwave were written in a dead language. I foraged for a single spoon to scoop out the pineapple. I ended up having to wait until Holly arrived to use one of her plastic spoons. (Remember when Alan Rickman threatened to carve someone's heart out with a spoon in *Robin Hood*? It can't be nearly as difficult as scooping out pineapple with a plastic spoon.) Out of sheer desperation, we called for Mary's help a few times for any sort of useful utensil—honestly, we would have taken a garden shovel, at this point—but all we got was radio silence, and we were left to MacGyver this meal on our own.

Ding.

The ham was done. Instinctually, I reached in the drawer for a pot holder. None. I looked around for a kitchen towel. None of those either. There was an episode of *The Office* when Steve Carell's character was pissed that he received a homemade pot holder during Secret Santa. If he was in my kitchen, I would have bitchslapped him.

In lieu of having any of my family members strip down in the middle of the kitchen so I could use their nice Easter outfits to coax a hot pig out of the oven, I ended up using the only thing available— aluminum foil and paper towels. Let me tell you, Brawny towels may be tough on messes, but they're a big wusses when it comes to handling scalding-hot dead pigs. The towels incinerated on impact and several layers of my epidermis were sacrificed to the all-mighty Easter ham. I was beginning to wonder if this meal qualified me for a Purple Heart.

Mary finally emerged after dinner was fully prepared. I was rewarded for my service by being forced to eat dinner on the floor. In a home where potholders are an endangered species, naturally there weren't enough chairs, either. As I sat on the hard floor gnawing on my Easter dinner that was flavored with my own burnt skin, I caught my sister Holly looking at me.

"I told you so," her eyes said.

If you happen to hear a news report this year about a woman who kidnapped her sister on Christmas Eve and fled the state, please don't look for them. Trust me—it's in the sister's best interest.

All Jessica Pinkman wants for Christmas is a mint chocolate martini IV to survive. Her hobbies include driving around the country in her rustbucketed RV. Next holiday, she plans to be driving it toward a beach with her kidnapped sister in the back.

Christ-mess Card
Robyn Renee Riley

Every year it's the same.

Some people fear getting trampled to death while Black Friday shopping.

Others stress about not finding whatever version of Elmo it is you are supposed to buy.

But, my greatest holiday fear?

The Christmas card.

I'm not talking about the boxes of Christmas cards you can go to any store and buy. That's easy. You decide if you want to be religious—Mary/Joseph/baby Jesus on front, or cute—a dog wearing reindeer antlers, or nothing with a generic "Happy Holidays."

I'm talking about the elusive photo Christmas card.

You see, before you have the photo Christmas card, you have to have the photo. The perfect family Christmas photo.

I figure I must be missing something. People must have better lives, better children, or better abilities at Photoshop.

I've been trying to get "the perfect Christmas card" for 6 years now.

When you live in the reality that is divorce and remarriage with kids, first you have to find a time when all of you are together.

This magical thing happened, when the planets aligned—not only were we all together, we were all in Church clothes. Of course, none of us matched in the slightest. I was wearing plaid. The teenage boy was sporting a retro cardigan. One girl was wearing a cherry print, and the other, floral. My husband, the Pastor, was in his clerical collar. I figured at best, our photo would come off as a nice minister who had stopped to help out a rag-tag bunch.

Thankfully, I had not allowed the youngest girl to wear what she wanted to wear that morning. Her idea of proper church attire? Leather shorts. Leg warmers. Long, feather earrings. And I quote her: "I can rock this look." No, dear. I'm pretty sure you can only "rock that look" if you are streetwalking. If you are a 12-year-old girl, you cannot rock that look. At least not under my watch!

I had the realization that we were not only all together, but half-way decently dressed, driving down the road. I told the Pastor we had to act fast. What happened next I'm sure was like having to race to get on the last helicopter out of Saigon. The Pastor pulled into a parking lot, screeched to a halt, and we all ran to take pictures outside. It was even a decent day weather-wise. With this series of events happening, we were either going to get the perfect family picture or the world was about to end. I checked my phone to see if this was one of those dates predicted for the rapture.

The Pastor hurriedly set up his tripod—yes, he carries it in his backpack all the time. We turned the timer on and just took shot after shot with the theory being we might get one decent picture.

Sure the 12-year-old had some moments when she completely forgot how to smile and was making weird looking faces. And the 14-year-old panicked at how to stand in front of the camera. And between each exposure, the Pastor and I were yelling at them, telling them to move here and there—screaming as though they might not make it aboard the helicopter and out of the war-torn country.

It doesn't end with the picture. Once you get that, you have to attempt to order the cards. Here's how that works. You go to various websites and look at design, after design, after design. There is an infinite number of possibilities. Cards range in price from roughly $0.01-$15.00 per card. Inevitably, the ones you will like will be the $15.00 cards. Once you find a card in your price range, it will need a vertical picture, and you will only have a good horizontal one. Or, it is a card that will hold four pictures, and you need five.

Once you have managed to find the one card out of 27,382 that has the layout and number of pictures you need, and doesn't say Happy Hannukuh (for a moment you will contemplate converting to Judaism, for it will make ordering cards easier) you will begin the process of dropping your pictures into the layout.

First you kiss your husband goodnight and grab an energy drink because you are in for an all-nighter. After you somehow manage to get the right pictures in the right slots, you have to put a message or your names in a text box. Whatever you want to say, or however many names you have, it will be too many letters. You will all of a sudden give one kid a nickname they've never had, because it will fit on the card. Don't even think about trying to change the font, you will want to get at least 30 minutes of sleep.

I'm not bragging here. I've got a college degree. I went to tech school for a year. I've given birth to a child. I've held professional jobs, including one that required me to manage and be responsible for a number of employees. Why is it so hard to order a Merry freakin' Christmas card?

You've managed to order the cards. Once they come in, you will be faced with the arduous task of addressing the envelopes. Your husband will ask you approximately every 30 minutes if "you've gotten the Christmas cards done." You know, in all your spare time.

You finally finish. Then comes the stamping, the return address labels, and the trip to the post office. Then over the next series of weeks, you will receive at least one returned in the mail every day because as it turns out you don't actually know where anyone lives.

But I did it. You'd think for this alone I'd deserve something extra special in my stocking this year. I know I'm not going to get any presents, so I'll just settle for never ever having to see the 12-year-old wear leather booty shorts and leg warmers.

Thanks, Santa.

Robyn Renee Riley is a humor writer who lives in Oklahoma. She lives with her husband the Pastor, a teenage son and two teenage step-daughters. She likes to wear false eyelashes, red lipstick, and high heels while writing about her adventures as a modern-day pastor's wife.

An Easter Basket Gone Wrong

Teresa Ambord

Being a mom has all kinds of pleasures...and all kinds of challenges. For me, one of the most persistent challenges was getting Ryan, my teenage son, to help around the house. My pet peeve has always been overflowing trash cans. And of course, Ryan could never remember to empty them. So if I saw one that had been overlooked, I'd set it outside his bedroom and rap on the door. He'd come out, see it, and with a great show of teenage huffing and puffing, he'd empty it. For me, that was a challenge.

Then there was one of my great pleasures of motherhood, the making of the Easter baskets through the years. When he was little, there was all that colorful cellophane, the small toys, candy, and Easter grass. It was all tucked into a flimsy straw basket that later, would get placed on a closet shelf and forgotten. As Ryan grew a bit older, the toys gave way to slightly more expensive gifts, but the cellophane and the candy remained. The flimsy straw baskets gave way to items that could hold a lot, but had other uses, too, like a giant mug for his water or a backpack stuffed with fun things.

One year, just before Easter, Ryan mentioned that he needed a trash can for his room. I had what I thought was a clever idea. I bought a small bright green trash can, and used it as his Easter basket. It was deep enough that it held a lot...some CDs, some new socks, a DVD he wanted, and of course, a lot of candy along with his favorite beef jerky.

On Easter morning I sat on the couch drinking coffee, waiting for Ryan to get up and find his Easter basket sitting outside his door. Finally I could wait no more. I went to his door and gave a quick knock, and then I returned to my place on the couch with my coffee. I could hear him rustling around. Any second, I thought, he'd appear with his Easter basket in hand and sit on the couch with me and explore the contents. That didn't happen. Half asleep, he'd stumbled to the door, opened it, and saw a small bright green trash can sitting there. Immediately he did what I'd trained him to do…he took it straight out the back door and emptied it into the big trash can. Then he came to find me in the living room.

"Where does this one go?" he asked, holding up the empty trash can.

All I could do was stare at him, with my mouth open. "What did you do? Where's the stuff that was in it?"

"I emptied it into the backyard trash," he said, sounding annoyed, like I was the densest parent on the planet. "Hey, it's Easter, don't I get an Easter basket?"

"That *was* your Easter basket," I told him. "It was literally packed full of goodies."

It took awhile, but Ryan was able to salvage most of the contents. Of course that meant getting down and dirty with the garbage…coffee grounds, egg shells, slimy butter wrappers, etc.

Ah well, that Easter was not easily forgotten. I still do corny things, but after that Easter, I gave up trying to be clever with Ryan.

The Christmas Pineapple
Winston Kidd

Bored is not a good state for me to be in. Not good for me, nor anyone around me for that matter.

When I was four, bored got me to convince my two friends to ford a creek to see what was beyond the highway on the other side of said creek (that was known to harbor alligators). Our parents found us only a few minutes after an observant Florida State Trooper did. To this day, I am convinced that we would have seen and out maneuvered any 'gators. (Four year-old me had much better Ninja moves than present-day me).

You might ask where my parents were while I was playing The Crocodile Hunter at four. Well, I was raised in a strict Irish-Catholic family. Which means, I was brought up on equal parts whiskey and guilt. It also means that I am one of many. Six to be exact. It should be noted that after the third child is born, the two parents have to switch from a man-to-man defense to a zone defense, and "Bored" had me frequently out of the zone.

Honestly after number four, parents are relegated to strictly 'triage' activities, and by number six, if the result does not involve bodily harm, chances are you are not going to get any attention at all. Surprisingly enough, we all survived, and one of the best things about a big family is Christmas!

Like many families, we had a number of traditions. My favorite was Christmas Eve when we would all go to midnight Mass, then come home, drink, and wrap presents in different rooms (so the recipient

remained unaware). For decades, this Just-In-Time tradition worked well, but as my older
siblings got married and had children of their own, this system began to become somewhat unwieldy. OK, it became total chaos.

One particular Christmas, I was "home" visiting the family. I put "home" in quotes because my family had moved from Massachusetts to New Jersey, so when I went "home," it wasn't. None of my friends lived around there, and I inevitably and quickly got 'Bored'. My mother, whose nerves were about as sturdy as the Chernobyl containment building at this point would try to get me to do things, so I would not be 'Bored' in front of her while she was trying to get things done.

(Note: This story takes place in the early 1980's. As hard as it is to believe, there was no internet, no XBoX 360, IPad, text messaging, or even cell phones at that time! Barbaric, I know.)

So during this particular Christmas, my mother threw money at me and told me to go grocery shopping. She handed me a list of about 20 items and then said the following words: "Make sure you get everything on the list, and anything else you can think of that we might need."

Let me assure you that "anything else you can think of" is far too much latitude to grant a teenaged me. I have a vivid imagination, which was born of necessity because in my younger years we traipsed around the country by car. I am talking New Jersey, to Florida, to Ohio, to Louisiana, and back again. Did I mention six kids, SIX!

We were packed in the car so tightly that folks from Mexico used to study our car as an example of how to sneak the maximum people over the border. (We received thank you notes from many of their 'customers'.)

As far as the "things that we might need" part goes, well, need is very subjective, I can make a case that we need almost anything, LIKE MORE ROOM on the ride from Jackson Mississippi to Pampano Beach, Florida, not that I am not holding a grudge.

Revenge notwithstanding, sending a 'bored' me to the grocery store with those instructions and someone else's money is a challenge, and I was not to disappoint.

As luck would have it, the store I entered had a special on whole pineapples. In my entire life, my family had never purchased a whole pineapple. Yet here it was, in all its natural beauty. Yes, I thought to myself, we NEEDED a pineapple, a Christmas Pineapple! So I bought two. The second one I planned to hide just in case my mother thought the idea of a Christmas Pineapple was crazy and threw the first one out. Yeah, I'm strategic like that.

I got home and the house was all abuzz. Nothing was really going on, but when you have a house that holds my grandparents, my parents, my three younger siblings, my older brother, his wife and child, and my oldest sister with her husband and their three kids, well abuzz just happens. I placed the Christmas Pineapple in the center of the dining room table where it was sure to get the level of attention that it deserved.

I retired to the TV room and like a master fisherman, waited for someone to take the bait. It did not take long for me to get the call.

"Wiiiiiinnnnnstonnnn!" my mother bellowed. "What is this?" she said as she held out the pineapple.

"Why that's a pineapple, Mom. You should know that," I replied, biting back the smile.

"I know it is a pineapple, Winston," She replied, not at all happy with my little game.

"Then why did you ask? You are not having a stroke are you?" I said, knowing that I had already crossed the line. Hell, once the little game has been started, you just have to finish it. That is one of the rules. Seriously, go look it up.

"I asked because I wanted to know what it is doing on the dining room table!" Mother said, the tone in her voice notably sharper now. (It should also be noted that at this point, I am smiling because I know I have a backup pineapple and the probability that this one winds up in the compactor is fast approaching 'one').

"Where did this come from?" she added, "And if you tell me Hawaii, I'm going to beat you with a wooden ladle!"

"The store, Mom. Where else?" I replied, knowing that she needed this little stress relief, even if she did not see it as such. OK, maybe I was just bored and this was a pleasant distraction.

"I did not tell you to buy a pineapple!" she demanded.

"Yes, you did! You said to buy anything else I thought we might need, and we need a Christmas pineapp—"

Before I could finish, my mother made off like a shot and threw the fruit into the compactor and promptly activated it. She stormed off in the direction of the dining room, mumbling something to herself about ungrateful children and not having enough to do, and other things that I was too busy snickering to myself to understand.

For those thinking I was being mean, fear not. In an extremely stressful situation, taking an action like smashing a defenseless pineapple, which you, yourself did not purchase, is a wonderful stress relief! You should really try it sometime and see for yourself.

Time for plan B! Plan B takes timing and patience. You must understand that one cannot just replace the original pineapple with the backup so soon after the original was disposed of. Psychologists say the subject needs a cooling off period before the introduction of the next 'stimulus'. Move too soon and the anger that precipitated the first disposal will just be employed to destroy the second. However, if you wait, then the person in question will need to go back up the anger curve and is more likely to just accept the new addition.

No, I am not a psychologist. Yes, I just made that entire thing up, and yes it did actually work out that way.

About two hours later, after dinner, and just about the time that Santa was hooking up the reindeer (despite PETA's best efforts mind you), the Christmas Pineapple reappeared on the dining room table.

As the family reconvened for dessert and pre-church drinks, my sister noticed the new table décor and asked: "Why is there a pineapple in the middle of the table?"

"That is a Christmas Pineapple," I respond, cutting off my mother.

"What on earth is a Christmas Pineapple?" my father asked.

I immediately felt a sense of victory followed by extreme panic. You see, having Dad ask the question is akin to international recognition of a new government. There is no undoing it; however, there needs to be an explanation—not a great one, but a decent one. There, I was a bit lacking. You see 'bored' me is not good at long-term planning. Fortunately, I have a wonderful imagination, forged over hours and days confined, oh wait, I already told you that part.

Fearlessly, I grabbed the floor and began my oration, making it up as I went.

"Way back when the missionaries first invaded, um, I mean settled with the natives on the big Island of Hawaii, they were trying to teach the natives about Jesus and Santa Claus. But due to the tropical climate, there were no conifers, no Christmas Trees. This made the people very sad. They had thought they could get around the problem of no chimneys by lighting fires, and they had erected large signs to warn Santa that Mt. Haleakala was a volcano, not a big chimney. But without Christmas Trees, they felt they were doomed! Just then, a flock of fireflies landed on a nearby pineapple and in a test of sexual dominance, they all lit at the same time, giving a wonderful glow to the fruit. The natives knew that this was a sign, and ever since that day, the Christmas Pineapple is treasured in each and every home. We have ours, to show solidarity with our poor brothers still living in Hawaii."

I wiped a tiny tear from my eye and looked out over my family...

"Bullshit!" exclaimed my father.

"I thought I already threw that away!" added my mother.

Just when it looked like my luck had run out, I quickly scanned the table for the pineapple, but it was gone. At that moment, in walks my older sister with a pitcher that contained the sacred innards of the Christmas Pineapple, floating in a clear liquid.

"That's a great idea, Winston!" she said. "Nothing like pineapples in vodka for a cold Christmas night!"

And the Christmas Pineapple is a family tradition to this very day!

Winston Kidd got divorced and decided to keep his talents in Andover, Massachusetts. There he lives with several spirits of unknown origin (according to a friend who claims she is 'sensitive'). Winston works for a small, conservative consulting company which shall remain nameless, at least until they go into receivership. When he is not experiencing life on the road, Winston likes to perform stand-up comedy.

Manufactured by Amazon.ca
Bolton, ON